JOHN PLOUGHMAN'S PICTURES

OR

MORE OF HIS PLAIN TALK FOR PLAIN PEOPLE

JOHN PLOUGHMAN'S PICTURES

OR

MORE OF HIS PLAIN TALK FOR PLAIN PEOPLE

by

C. H. SPURGEON

CHRISTIAN FOCUS PUBLICATIONS LTD.

This edition
© 1989 Christian Focus Publications Ltd.

ISBN 1 871676 231

Printed and bound in Great Britain by
Courier International Ltd, Tiptree, Essex

CONTENTS

6

LIST OF ILLUSTRATIONS

PREFACE

" JOHN PLOUGHMAN'S TALK" has not only obtained an immense circulation, but it has exercised an influence for good. Although its tone is rather moral than religious, it has led many to take the first steps by which men climb to better things, and this fact has moved me to attempt a second book of the same character. I have continued to use the simplest form of our mother tongue, so that if any readers must need have refined language they had better leave these pages before they are quite disgusted. To smite evil—and especially the monster evil of drink—has been my earnest endeavour, and assuredly there is need. It may be that the vice of drunkenness is not more common than it used to be; but it is sufficiently rampant to cause sorrow in every Christian bosom, and to lead all lovers of their race to lift up their voices against it. I hope that the plain speech of JOHN PLOUGHMAN will help in that direction.

It is quite out of the question for the compiler of such proverbial talk as this to acknowledge the sources from which the quaint sayings have been derived, for they are too numerous. I have gathered expressions and verses here, there, and everywhere; and perhaps the most simple way is to deny all claim to originality, and confess myself a gatherer of other men's stuffs. It is not quite so, but that is near enough. I have, however, borrowed many rhymes from "Thomas Tusser's Points of Good Husbandry," a book which is out of date, and forgotten, and never likely to be reprinted.

I have somewhat indulged the mirthful vein, but ever with so serious a purpose that I ask no forgiveness. Those who see a virtue in dulness have full permission to condemn, for a sufficient number will approve.

May the kindness shown to the former volume be extended to this also.

C. H. SPURGEON

IF THE CAP FITS, WEAR IT

FRIENDLY READERS,

Last time I made a book I trod on some people's corns and bunions, and they wrote me angry letters, asking, "Did you mean me?" This time, to save them the expense of a halfpenny card, I will begin my book by saying—

> Whether I please or whether I tease,
>   I'll give you my honest mind;
> If the cap should fit, pray wear it a bit,
>   If not, you can leave it behind.

No offence is meant; but if anything in these pages should come home to a man, let him not send it next door, but get a coop for his own chickens. What is the use of reading or hearing for other people? We do not eat and drink for them: why should we lend them our ears and not our mouths? Please then, good friend, if you find a hoe on these premises, weed your own garden with it.

I was speaking with Will Shepherd the other day about our master's old donkey, and I said, "He is so old and stubborn, he really is not worth his keep." "No," said Will, "and worse still, he is so vicious, that I feel sure he'll do somebody a mischief one of these days." You know they say that walls have ears; we were talking rather loud, but we did not know that there were ears to haystacks. We stared, I tell you, when we saw Joe Scroggs come from behind the stack, looking as red as a turkey-cock, and raving like mad. He burst out swearing at Will and me, like a cat spitting at a dog. His monkey was up and no mistake. He'd let us know that he was as good a man as either of us, or the two put together, for the matter of that. Talking about *him* in that way; he'd do—I don't know what. I told old Joe we had never thought of him, nor said a word about him, and he might just as well save his breath to cool his porridge, for nobody meant him any harm. This only made him call me a liar, and roar the louder. My friend, Will, was walking away, holding his sides, but when he saw that Scroggs was still in a fume, he laughed outright, and turned round on him and said, "Why, Joe, we were talking about master's old donkey, and not about you; but, upon my word, I shall never see that donkey again without thinking of Joe Scroggs." Joe puffed and blowed, but perhaps he thought it an awkward job, for he backed out of it, and Will and I went off to our work in rather a merry cue, for old Joe had blundered on the truth about himself for once in his life.

The aforesaid Will Shepherd has sometimes come down rather heavy upon me in his remarks, but it has done me good. It is partly through his home thrusts that I have come to write this new book, for he thought I was idle; perhaps I am, and perhaps I am not. Will forgets that I have other fish to fry and tails to butter; and he does not recollect that a ploughman's mind wants to lie fallow a little, and can't give a crop every year. It is hard to make rope when your hemp is all used up, or pancakes without batter, or rook pie without the birds; and so I found it hard to write more when I had said just about all I knew. Giving much to the poor doth increase a man's store, but it is not the same with writing; at least, I am such a poor scribe that I don't find it comes because I pull. If your thoughts only flow by drops, you can't pour them out in bucketfuls.

However, Will has ferreted me out, and I am obliged to him so far. I told him the other day, what the winkle said to the pin: "Thank you for drawing me out, but you are rather sharp about it." Still, Master Will is not far from the mark: after three hundred thousand people had bought my book it certainly was time to write another: so, though I am not a hatter, I will again turn cap-maker, and those who have heads may try on my wares; those who have none won't touch them.

So, friends,
I am,
Yours, rough and ready,
JOHN PLOUGHMAN

BURN A CANDLE AT BOTH ENDS, AND IT WILL SOON BE GONE

WELL may he scratch his head who burns his candle at both ends; but, do what he may, his light will soon be gone, and he will be all in the dark. Young Jack Careless squandered his property, and now he is without a shoe to his foot. His was a case of "easy come, easy go: soon gotten, soon spent." He that earns an estate will keep it better than he that inherits it. As the Scotchman says, "He that gets gear before he gets wit is but a short time master of it," and so it was with Jack. His money burnt holes in his pocket. He could not get rid of it fast enough himself, and so he got a pretty set to help him, which they did by helping themselves. His fortune went like a pound of meat in a kennel of hounds. He was everybody's friend, and now he is everybody's fool.

He came in to old Alderman Greedy's money, for he was his nephew; but, as the old saying is, the fork followed the rake, the spender was heir to the hoarder. God has been very merciful to some of us in never letting money come rolling in upon us, for most men are carried off their legs if they meet with a great wave of fortune. Many of us would have been bigger sinners if we had been trusted with larger purses. Poor Jack had plenty of pence, but little sense. Money is easier made than made use of. What is hard to gather is easy to scatter. The old gentleman had lined his nest well, but Jack made the feathers fly like flakes of snow in winter-time. He got rid of his money by shovelfuls and then by cartloads. After spending the interest, he began swallowing the capital, and so killed the goose that laid the golden eggs. He squandered his silver and gold, in ways which must never be told. It would not go fast enough, so he bought race-horses to run away with it. He got into the hands of blacklegs, and fell into company of which we shall say but little; only when such madams smile, men's purses weep; these are a well without a bottom, and the more a fool throws in, the more he may. The greatest beauty often causes the greatest ruin. Play, women, and wine are enough to make a prince a pauper.

Always taking out and never putting back soon empties the biggest sack, and so Jack found it; but he took no notice till his last shilling bade him good-bye, and then he said he had been robbed; like silly Tom who put his finger in the fire and said it was his bad luck.

> His money once flashed like dew in the sun;
> When bills became due, of cash he had none.

"Drink and let drink" was his motto; every day was a holiday and every holiday was a feast. The best of wines and the dearest of dainties suited his tooth, for he meant to lead a pig's life, which they say is short and sweet. Truly, he went the whole hog. The old saying is, "a glutton young, a beggar old," and he seemed set upon proving it true. A fat kitchen makes a lean will; but he can make his will on his finger-nail, and leave room for a dozen codicils. In fact, he will never want a will at all, for he will leave nothing behind him but old scores. Of all his estate there is not enough left to bury him with. What he threw away in his prosperity would have kept a coat on his back and a dumpling in his pot to his life's end; but he never looked beyond his nose, and he could not see to the end of that. He laughed at prudence, and now prudence frowns at him. Punishment is lame, but it comes at last. He pays the cost of his folly in body and in soul, in purse and in person, and yet he is still a fool, and would dance to the same tune again if he had another chance. His light purse brings him a heavy heart, but he couldn't have his cake and eat it too. As he that is drunk at night is dry in the morning, so he that lavished money when he had it feels the want of it all the more when it is gone. His old friends have quite dropped him; they have squeezed the orange, and now they throw away the peel. As well look for milk from a pigeon as help from a fellow who loved you for your beer. Pot friends will let you go to pot, and kick you when you are down.

Jack has worse wants than the want of money, for his character is gone, and he is like a rotten nut, not worth the cracking: the neighbours say he is a ne'er-do-well, not worth calling out of a cabbage garden. Nobody will employ him, for he would not earn his salt, and so he goes from pillar to post, and has not a place to lay his head in. A good name is better than a girdle of gold, and when that is gone, what has a man left?

What has he left? Nothing upon earth! Yet the prodigal son has still a Father in heaven. Let him arise

and go to him, ragged as he is. He may smell of the
swine-trough, and yet he may run straight home, and
he shall not find the door locked. The great Father
will joyfully meet him, and kiss him, and cleanse him,
and clothe him, and give him to begin a new and
better life. When a sinner is at his worst he is not too
bad for the Saviour, if he will but turn from his wickedness and cry unto God for mercy. It's a long lane that
has no turning, but the best of all turns is to turn unto
the Lord with all your heart. This the great Father
will help the penitent prodigal to do. If the candle
has been burned all away, the Sun in the heavens is
still alight. Look, poor profligate: look to Jesus, and
live. His salvation is without money and without price.
Though you may not have a penny to bless yourself
with, the Lord Jesus will bless you freely. The depths
of your misery are not so deep as the depth of God's
mercy. If you are faithful and just in confessing the
sins you would have forgiven, God will be faithful
and just in forgiving the sins which you confess.

But, pray, do not go on another day as you are, for
this very day may be your last. If you will not heed a
plain word from John Ploughman, which he means
for your good, yet recollect this old-fashioned rhyme,
which was copied from a grave-stone:

> The loss of gold is great,
> The loss of health is more,
> But the loss of Christ is such a loss
> As no man can restore.

HUNCHBACK SEES NOT HIS OWN HUMP, BUT HE SEES HIS NEIGHBOUR'S

HE points at the man in front of him, but he is a good deal more of a guy himself. He should not laugh at the crooked until he is straight himself, and not then. I hate to hear a raven croak at a crow for being black. A blind man should not blame his brother for squinting, and he who has lost his legs should not sneer at the lame. Yet so it is, the rottenest bough cracks first, and he who should be the last to speak is the first to rail. Bespattered hogs bespatter others, and he who is full of fault finds fault. They are most apt to speak ill of others who do most ill themselves.

> "We're very keen our neighbour's hump to see,
>   We're blind to that upon our back alone;
> E'en though the lump far greater be,
>   It still remains to us unknown."

It does us much hurt to judge our neighbours, because it flatters our conceit, and our pride grows quite fast enough without feeding. We accuse others to excuse ourselves. We are such fools as to dream that we are better because others are worse, and we talk as if we could get up by pulling others down. What is the good of spying holes in people's coats when we can't mend them? Talk of my debts if you mean to pay them; if not, keep your red rag behind your ivory ridge. A friend's faults should not be advertised, and even a stranger's

should not be published. He who brays at an ass is an
ass himself, and he who makes a fool of another is a
fool himself. Don't get into the habit of laughing at
people, for the old saying is, "Hanging's stretching and
mocking's catching."

> Some must have their joke whoever they poke;
> For the sake of fun mischief is done,
> And to air their wit full many they hit.

Jesting is too apt to turn into jeering, and what was
meant to tickle makes a wound. It is a pity when my
mirth is another man's misery. Before a man cracks a
joke he should consider how he would like it himself,
for many who give rough blows have very thin skins.
Give only what you would be willing to take: some men
throw salt on others, but they smart if a pinch of it
falls on their own raw places. When they get a Roland
for their Oliver, or a tit for their tat, they don't like it;
yet nothing is more just. Biters deserve to be bitten.

We may chide a friend, and so prove our friendship,
but it must be done very daintily, or we may lose our
friend for our pains. Before we rebuke another we must
consider, and take heed that we are not guilty of the
same thing, for he who cleanses a blot with inky fingers
makes it worse. To despise others is a worse fault than
any we are likely to see in them, and to make merry
over their weaknesses shows our own weakness and our
own malice too. Wit should be a shield for defence,
and not a sword for offence. A mocking word cuts
worse than a scythe, and the wound is harder to heal.
A blow is much sooner forgotten than a jeer. Mocking
is shocking. Our minister says "to laugh at infirmity

or deformity is an enormity." He is a man who ought to know a thing or two, and he puts a matter as pat as butter.

> "Who ridicules his neighbour's frailty
>   Scoffs at his own in more or less degree:
>   Much wiser he who others' lets alone,
>   And tries his hardest to correct his own."

IT IS HARD FOR AN EMPTY SACK TO
STAND UPRIGHT

SAM may try a fine while before he will make one of his empty sacks stand upright. If he were not half daft he would have left off that job before he began it, and not have been an Irishman either. He will come to his wit's end before he sets the sack on its end. The old proverb, printed at the top, was made by a man who had burnt his fingers with debtors, and it just means that when folks have no money and are over head and ears in debt, as often as not they leave off being upright, and tumble over one way or another. He that has but four and spends five will soon need no purse, but he will most likely begin to use his wits to keep himself afloat, and take to all sorts of dodges to manage it.

Nine times out of ten they begin by making promises to pay on a certain day when it is certain they have nothing to pay with. They are as bold at fixing the time as if they had my lord's income: the day comes round as sure as Christmas, and then they haven't a penny-piece in the world, and so they make all sorts of excuses and begin to promise again. Those who are quick to promise are generally slow to perform. They promise mountains and perform mole-hills. He who gives you fair words and nothing more feeds you with an empty spoon, and hungry creditors soon grow tired of that game. Promises don't fill the belly. Promis-

ing men are not great favorites if they are not performing
men. When such a fellow is called a liar he thinks he is
hardly done by; and yet he is so, as sure as eggs are
eggs, and there's no denying it, as the boy said when
the gardener caught him up the cherry tree. People
don't think much of a man's piety when his promises
are like pie-crust, made to be broken: they generally
turn crusty themselves and give him a bit of their mind.
Like old Tusser, who said of such an one:

> "His promise to trust to is slippery as ice,
> His credit much like to the chance of the dice."

Creditors have better memories than debtors, and when
they have been taken in more than once they think it is
time that the fox went to the furrier, and they had their
share of his skin. Waiting for your money does not
sweeten a man's temper, and a few lies on the top of it
turn the milk of human kindness into sour stuff. Here
is an old-fashioned saying which a bad payer may put
in his pipe, and smoke or not, as he likes:

> "He that promiseth till no man will trust him,
> He that lieth till no man will believe him,
> He that borroweth till no man will lend him,
> Let him go where no man knoweth him."

Hungry dogs will eat dirty puddings, and people who
are hard up very often do dirty actions. Blessed be God,
there is some cloth still made which will not shrink
in the wetting, and some honesty which holds on under
misfortune; but too often debt is the worst kind of
poverty, because it breeds deceit. Men do not like to

face their circumstances, and so they turn their backs
on the truth. They try all sorts of schemes to get out of
their difficulties, and like the Banbury tinker, they
make three holes in the saucepan to mend one. They
are like Pedley, who burnt a penny candle in looking
for a farthing. They borrow of Peter to pay Paul, and
then Peter is let in for it. To avoid a brook they leap
into a river, for they borrow at ruinous interest to pay
off those who squeeze them tight. By ordering goods
which they cannot pay for, and selling them for whatever they can get, they may put off one evil day, but
they only bring on another. One trick needs another
trick to back it up, and thus they go on over shoes and
then over boots. Hoping that something will turn up,
they go on raking for the moon in a ditch, and all the
luck that comes to them is like Johnny Toy's, who lost
a shilling and found a two-penny loaf. Any short cut
tempts them out of the high road of honesty, and they
find after a while that they have gone miles out of their
way. At last people fight shy of them, and say that they
are as honest as a cat when the meat is out of reach,
and they murmur that plain dealing is dead, and died
without issue. Who wonders? People who are bitten
once are in no hurry to put their fingers into the same
mouth again. You don't trust a horse's heel after it has
kicked you, nor lean on a staff which has once broken.
Too much cunning overdoes its work, and in the
long run there is no craft which is so wise as simple
honesty.

I would not be hard on a poor fellow, nor pour
water on a drowned mouse: if through misfortune the
man can't pay, why he can't pay, and let him say so,

and do the honest thing with what little he has, and kind hearts will feel for him. A wise man does at first what a fool does at last. The worst of it is, that debtors will hold on long after it is honest to do so, and they try to persuade themselves that their ship will come home, or their cats will grow into cows. It is hard to sail over the sea in an egg-shell, and it is not much easier to pay your way when your capital is all gone. Out of nothing comes nothing, and you may turn your nothing over a long time before it will grow into a ten-pound note. The way to Babylon will never bring you to Jerusalem, and borrowing, and diving deeper into debt, will never get a man out of difficulties.

The world is a ladder for some to go up and some to go down, but there is no need to lose your character because you lose your money. Some people jump out of the frying-pan into the fire; for fear of being paupers they become rogues. You find them slippery customers; you can't bind them to anything: you think you have got them, but you can't hold them any longer than you can keep a cat in a wheelbarrow. They can jump over nine hedges, and nine more after that. They always deceive you, and then plead the badness of the times, or the sickness of their family. You cannot help them, for there's no telling where they are. It is always best to let them come to the end of their tether, for when they are cleaned out of their old rubbish they may perhaps begin in a better fashion. You cannot get out of a sack what is not in it, and when a man's purse is as bare as the back of your hand, the longer you patch him up the barer he will become, like Bill Bones, who cut up his coat to patch his waistcoat, and then used his trousers to mend his coat, and at last had to lie in bed for want of a rag to cover him.

Let the poor, unfortunate tradesman hold to his honesty as he would to his life. The straight road is the shortest cut. Better break stones on the road than break the law of God. Faith in God should save a Christian man from anything like a dirty action; let him not even think of playing a trick, for you cannot touch pitch without being defiled therewith. Christ and a crust is riches, but a broken character is the worst of bankruptcy. All is not lost while uprightness remains; but still *it is hard to make an empty sack stand upright*.

There are other ways of using the old saying. It is hard for a hypocrite to keep up his profession. Empty sacks can't stand upright in a church any better than in a granary. Prating does not make saints, or there would be plenty of them. Some talkatives have not religion enough to flavour soup for a sick grasshopper, and they have to be mighty cunning to keep the game going. Long prayers and loud professions only deceive the simple, and those who see further than the surface soon spy out the wolf under the sheepskin.

All hope of salvation by our own good works is a foolish attempt to make an empty sack stand upright. We are undeserving, ill-deserving, hell-deserving sinners at the best. The law of God must be kept without a single failure if we hope to be accepted by it; but there is not one among us who has lived a day without sin. No, we are a lot of empty sacks, and unless the merits of Christ are put into us to fill us up, we cannot stand in the sight of God. The law condemns us already, and to hope for salvation by it is to run to the gallows to prolong our lives. There is a full Christ for empty sinners, but those who hope to fill themselves will find their hopes fail them.

HE WHO WOULD PLEASE ALL WILL
LOSE HIS DONKEY AND BE LAUGHED AT
FOR HIS PAINS

HERE'S a queer picture, and this is the story which goes with it; you shall have it just as I found it in an old book. "An old man and his young son were driving an ass before them to the next market to sell. 'Why have you no more wit,' says one to the man upon the way, 'than you and your son to trudge it a-foot, and let the ass go light?' So the old man set his son upon the ass, and footed it himself. 'Why, sirrah,' says another after this to the boy, 'ye lazy rogue, you, must you ride, and let your old father go a-foot?' The old man upon this took down his son, and got up himself. 'Do you see,' says a third, 'how the lazy old knave rides himself, and the poor young fellow has much ado to creep after him?' The father, upon this, took up his son behind him. The next they met asked the old man whether the ass were his own or no? He said, 'Yes.' 'Troth, there's little sign on't,' says the other, 'by your loading him thus.' 'Well,' says the old man to himself, 'and what am I to do now? for I'm laughed at, if either the ass be empty, or if *one* of us rides, or *both*:' and so he came to the conclusion to bind the ass's legs together with a cord, and they tried to carry him to market with a pole upon their shoulders, betwixt them. This was sport to everybody that saw it, inasmuch that the old man in great wrath

" The old man and his donkey."

threw down the ass into a river, and so went his way home again. The good man, in fine, was willing to please everybody, but had the ill fortune to please nobody, and lost his ass into the bargain."

He who will not go to bed till he pleases everybody will have to sit up a great many nights. Many men, many minds; many women, many whims; and so if we please one we are sure to set another grumbling. We had better wait till they are all of one mind before we mind them, or we shall be like the man who hunted many hares at once and caught none. Besides, the fancies of men alter, and folly is never long pleased with the same thing, but changes its palate, and grows sick of what it doted on. Will Shepherd says he once tried to serve two masters, but, says he, "I soon had enough of it, and I declared that, if I was pardoned this once, the next time they caught me at it they might pickle me in salt and souse me in boiling vinegar."

> "He who would general favour win
> And not himself offend,
> To-day the task he may begin,
> He'll never, never end."

If we dance to every fiddle we shall soon be lame in both legs. Good nature may be a great misfortune if we do not mix prudence with it.

> He that all men would please
> Shall never find ease.

It is right to be obliging, but we are not obliged to be every man's lackey. Put your hand quickly to your hat, for that is courtesy; but don't bow your head at every man's bidding, for that is slavery. He who hopes to please all should first fit the moon with a suit of clothes, or fill a bottomless barrel with buckets with their hoops off. To live upon the praises of others is to feed on the air; for what is praise but the breath of men's nostrils? That's poor stuff to make a dinner of. To set traps for claps, and to faint if you don't get them, is a childish thing; and to change your coat to please new company is as mean as dirt. Change for the better as often as you like, but mind it is better before you change. Tom of Bedlam never did a madder thing than he who tried to please a thousand masters at once: one is quite enough. If a man pleases God he may let the world wag its own way, and frown or flatter, as the maggot bites. What is there, after all, to frighten a man in a fool's grin, or in the frown of a poor mortal like yourself? If it mattered at all what the world says of us, it would be some comfort that when a good man is buried people say, "He was not a bad fellow after all." When the cow is dead we hear how much milk she gave. When the man's gone to heaven folks know their loss, and wonder how it was they did not treat him better.

The way of pleasing men is hard, but blessed are they who please God. He is not a free man who is afraid to think for himself, for if his thoughts are in bonds the man is not free. A man of God is a manly man. A true man does what he thinks to be right, whether the pigs grunt or the dogs howl. Are you afraid to follow out your conscience because Tom, Jack, and Harry, or Mary Ann and Betsy, would laugh at you? Then you are not the seventy-fifth cousin to John

Ploughman, who goes on his way whistling merrily, though many find fault with himself, and his plough, and his horses, and his harness, and his boots, and his coat, and his waistcoat, and his hat, and his head, and every hair on it. John says it amuses them and doesn't hurt him; but depend on it you will never catch John or his boys carrying the donkey.

ALL ARE NOT HUNTERS THAT BLOW
THE HORN

H E is not much like a hunter! Nimrod would never own him. But how he blows! Goodness, gracious, what a row! as the linnet said when he heard a donkey singing his evening hymn. There's more goes to ploughing than knowing how to whistle, and hunting is not all tally-ho and horn-blowing. Appearances are deceitful. Outward show is not everything. All are not butchers that carry a steel, and all are not bishops that wear aprons. You must not buy goods by the label; for I have heard that the finer the trade-mark the worse the article. Blow away, my hearty, till your toes look out of your boots; there's no fear of your killing either fox or stag!

Now, the more people blow, the more they may, but he is a fool who believes all they say. As a rule, the smallest boy carries the biggest fiddle, and he who makes most boast has least roast. He who has least wisdom has most vanity. John Lackland is wonderfully fond of being called Esquire, and there's none so pleased at being dubbed a doctor as the man who least deserves it. Many a D.D. is fiddle-dee-dee. I have heard say, "Always talk big and somebody will think you great," but my old friend Will Shepherd says, "Save your wind for running up a hill, and don't give us big words off a weak stomach. Look," said he once to me, "There's Solomon Braggs holding up his head like a hen drinking

water, but there's nothing in it. With him it's much
din and little done."

> "Of all speculations the market holds forth,
>   The best that I know for a lover of pelf,
>   Were to buy up this Braggs at the price he is worth,
>   And sell him—at that which he sets on himself."

Before honour is humility, but a prating fool shall
fall, and when he falls very few will be in a hurry to
pick him up.

A long tongue generally goes with a short hand.
We are most of us better at saying than doing. We can
all tattle away from the battle, but many fly when the
fight is nigh. Some are all sound and fury, and when
they have bragged their brag all is over, and *amen*.
The fat Dutchman was the wisest pilot in Flushing,
only he never went to sea; and the Irishman was the
finest rider in Connaught, only he would never trust
himself on a horse, because, as he said, "he generally
fell off before he got on." A bachelor's wife is always
well managed, and old maids always bring up their
children in prime style. We think we can do what we
are not called to, and if by chance the thing falls to
our lot we do worse than those we blamed. Hence it is
wise to be slow in foretelling what we will do, for—

> "Thus saith the proverb of the wise,
>   'Who boasteth least tells fewest lies.' "

There is another old rhyme which is as full of reason
as a pod is full of peas:

> "Little money is soonest spended;
>   Fewest words are soonest mended."

Of course, every potter praises his own pot, and we can all toot a little on our own trumpet, but some blow as if nobody ever had a horn but themselves. "After me the flood," says the mighty big man, and whether it be so or no we have floods enough while he lives. I mean floods of words, words, words, enough to drown all your senses. O that the man had a mouth big enough to say all he has to say at one go, and have done with it; but then one had need get to the other end of the world till his talk had run itself dry. O for a quiet hay-loft, or a saw-pit, or a dungeon, where the sound of the jawbone would no more be heard. They say a brain is worth little if you have not a tongue; but what is a tongue worth without a brain? Bellowing is all very well, but the cow for me is that which fills the pail. A braying ass eats little hay, and that's a saving in fodder; but a barking dog catches no game, and that's a loss to the owner. Noise is no profit, and talk hinders work.

When a man's song is in his praise, let the hymn be short metre, and let the tune be in the minor key. He who talks for ever about himself has a foolish subject, and is likely to worry and weary all around him. Good wine needs no bush, and a man who can do well seldom boasts about it. The emptiest tub makes the loudest noise. Those who give themselves out to be fine shots kill very few birds, and many a crack ploughman does a shorter day's work than plain John, though he is nothing off the common; and so on the whole it is pretty clear that the best huntsmen are not those who are for everlastingly blowing the horn.

A HANDSAW IS A GOOD THING, BUT NOT TO SHAVE WITH

OUR friend will cut more than he will eat, and shave off something more than hair, and then he will blame the saw. His brains don't lie in his beard, nor yet in the skull above it, or he would see that his saw will only make sores. There's sense in choosing your tools, for a pig's tail will never make a good arrow, nor will his ear make a silk purse. You can't catch rabbits with drums, nor pigeons with plums. A good thing is not good out of its place. It is much the same with lads and girls; you can't put all boys to one trade, nor send all girls to the same service. One chap will make a London clerk, and another will do better to plough, and sow, and reap, and mow, and be a farmer's boy. It's no use forcing them; a snail will never run a race, nor a mouse drive a waggon.

> "Send a boy to the well against his will,
> The pitcher will break and the water spill."

With unwilling hounds it is hard to hunt hares. To go against nature and inclination is to row against wind and tide. They say you may praise a fool till you make him useful: I don't know so much about that, but I do know that if I get a bad knife I generally cut my finger, and a blunt axe is more trouble than profit. No, let me shave with a razor if I shave at all, and do my work with the best tools I can get.

Never set a man to work he is not fit for, for he will never do it well. They say that if pigs fly they always go with their tails forward, and awkward workmen are much the same. Nobody expects cows to catch crows, or hens to wear hats. There's reason in roasting eggs, and there should be reason in choosing servants. Don't put a round peg into a square hole, nor wind up your watch with a cork-screw, nor set a tender-hearted man to whip wife-beaters, nor a bear to be a relieving-officer, nor a publican to judge of the licensing laws. Get the right man in the right place, and then all goes as smooth as skates on ice; but the wrong man puts all awry, as the sow did when she folded the linen.

It is a temptation to many to trust them with money: don't put them to take care of it if you ever wish to see it again. Never set a cat to watch cream, nor a pig to gather peaches, for if the cream and the peaches go a-missing you will have yourself to thank for it. It is a sin to put people where they are likely to sin. If you believe the old saying that when you set a beggar on horseback he will ride to the devil, don't let him have a horse of yours.

If you want a thing well done do it yourself, and pick your tools. It is true that a man must row with such oars as he has, but he should not use the boat-hook for a paddle. Take not the tongs to poke the fire, nor the poker to put on the coals. A newspaper on Sunday is as much out of place as a warming-pan on the first of August, or a fan on a snowy day: the Bible suits the Sabbath a deal better.

He who tries to make money by betting uses a wrong tool, and is sure to cut his fingers. As well hope to grow golden pippins on the bottom of the sea as to make gain among gamblers if you are an honest man. Hard work and thrifty habits are the right razor, gambling is a handsaw.

Some things want doing gently, and telling a man of his faults is one of them. You would not fetch a hatchet to break open an egg, nor kill a fly on your boy's forehead with a sledge-hammer, and so you must not try to mend your neighbour's little fault by blowing him up sky-high. Never fire off a musket to kill a midge, and don't raise a hue and cry about the half of nothing.

Do not throw away a saw because it is not a razor, for it will serve your turn another day, and cut your ham-bone if it won't shave off your stubble. A whetstone, though it cannot cut, may sharpen a knife that will. A match gives little light itself, but it may light a candle to brighten up the room. Use each thing and each man according to common sense and you will be uncommonly sensible. You don't milk horses nor ride cows, and by the same rule you must make of every man what he is meant for, and the farm will be as right as a trivet.

Everything has its use, but no one thing is good for all purposes. The baby said, "The cat crew and the cock rocked the cradle," but old folks knew better: the cat is best at mousing and the cock at rousing. That's for that, as salt is for herrings, and sugar for gooseberries, and Nan for Nicholas. Don't choose your tools by their looks, for that's best which does best. A silver trowel lays very few bricks. You cannot curry a horse with a tortoiseshell comb, or fell oaks with a pen-knife, or open oysters with a gold tooth-pick. *Fine* is not so good

given himself a box on the ear in his blind rage, aye, and ended his own life out of spite. He who cannot curb his temper carries gunpowder in his bosom, and he is neither safe for himself nor his neighbours. When passion comes in at the door, what little sense there is indoors flies out at the window. By-and-by a hasty man cools and comes to himself, like MacGibbon's gruel when he put it out of the window, but if his nose is off in the meantime, who is to put it on again? He will only be sorry once and that will be all the rest of his life. Anger does a man more hurt than that which made him angry. It opens his mouth and shuts his eyes, and fires his heart, and drowns his sense, and makes his wisdom folly. Old Tompkins told me that he was sorry that he lost his temper, and I could not help thinking that the pity was that he ever found it again, for it was like an old shoe with the sole gone and the upper leathers worn out, only fit for a dunghill. A hot tempered man would be all the better for a new heart, and a right spirit. Anger is a fire which cooks no victuals, and comforts no household: it cuts and curses and kills, and no one knows what it may lead to; therefore, good reader, don't let it lodge in your bosom, and if it ever comes there, pass the vagrant on to the next parish.

> Gently, gently, little pot,
> Why so hasty to be hot?
> Over you will surely boil,
> And I know not what you'll spoil.

The old gent has a fine nose of his own, and though he will be a fool to cut it off, he would be wise to cut off the supplies which have made it such a size. That glass and jug on the table are the paint-pots that he colours his nose with, and everybody knows, whether he knows it or knows it not, that his nose is the outward and visible sign of a good deal of inward and spirituous drink, and the sooner he drops his drops the better. So here we will cut off, not our nose, but the present subject.

HE HAS A HOLE UNDER HIS NOSE AND HIS MONEY RUNS INTO IT

THIS is the man who is always dry, because he takes so much heavy wet. He is a loose fellow who is fond of getting tight. He is no sooner up than his nose is in the cup, and his money begins to run down the hole which is just under his nose. He is not a blacksmith, but he has a spark in his throat, and all the publican's barrels can't put it out. If a pot of beer is a yard of land, he must have swallowed more acres than a ploughman could get over for many a day, and still he goes on swallowing until he takes to wallowing. All goes down Gutter Lane. Like the snipe, he lives by suction. If you ask him how he is, he says he would be quite right if he could moisten his mouth. His purse is a bottle, his bank is the publican's till, and his casket is a cask: pewter is his precious metal, and his pearl* is a mixture of gin and beer. The dew of his youth comes from Ben Nevis, and the comfort of his soul is cordial gin. He is a walking barrel, a living drain-pipe, a moving swill-tub. They say "loth to drink and loth to leave off," but he never needs persuading to begin, and as to ending—that is out of the question while he can borrow two-pence. This is the gentleman who sings—

> He that buys land buys many stones,
> He that buys meat buys many bones,

* Purl

> He that buys eggs buys many shells,
> He that buys good ale buys nothing else.

He will never be hanged for leaving his drink behind him. He drinks in season and out of season: in summer because he is hot, and in winter because he is cold. A drop of beer never comes too soon, and he would get up in the middle of the night for more, only he goes to bed too tipsy. He has heard that if you get wet-footed a glass of whisky in your boots will keep you from catching cold, and he argues that the best way to get one glass of the spirit into each boot is to put two doses where it will run into your legs. He is never long without an excuse for another pot, or if perchance he does not make one, another lushington helps him.

> Some drink when friends step in,
> And some when they step out;
> Some drink because they're thin,
> And some because they're stout.
>
> Some drink because 'tis wet,
> And some because 'tis dry;
> Some drink another glass
> To wet the other eye.

Water is this gentleman's abhorrence, whether used inside or out, but most of all he dreads it taken inwardly, except with spirits, and then the less the better. He says that the pump would kill him, but he never gives it a chance. He laps his liquor, and licks his chaps, but he will never die through the badness of the water from the well. It is a pity that he does not run the risk. Drinking cold water neither makes a man sick, nor in debt, nor his wife a widow, but this mighty fine ale of his will do all this for him, make him worse than a beast while he lives, and wash him away to his grave before his time. The old Scotchman said, "Death and drink-draining are near neighbours," and he spoke the truth. They say that drunkenness makes some men fools, some beasts, and some devils, but according to my mind it makes all men fools whatever else it does. Yet when a man is as drunk as a rat he sets up to be a judge, and mocks at sober people. Certain neighbours of mine laugh at me for being a teetotaller, and I might well laugh at them for being drunk, only I feel more inclined to cry that they should be such fools. O that we could get them sober, and then perhaps we might make men of them. You cannot do much with these fellows, unless you can enlist them in the Coldstream guards.

> He that any good would win
> At his mouth must first begin.

As long as drink drowns conscience and reason, you might as well talk to the hogs. The rascals will promise fair and take the pledge, and then take their coats to pledge to get more beer. We smile at a tipsy man, for he is a ridiculous creature, but when we see how he is ruined body and soul it is no joking matter. How solemn is the truth that "No drunkard shall inherit eternal life."

There's nothing too bad for a man to say or do when he is half-seas over. It is a pity that any decent body should go near such a common sewer. If he does not fall into the worst of crimes it certainly is not his fault, for he has made himself ready for anything the devil likes to put into his mind. He does least hurt when he begins to be topheavy, and to reel about: then he becomes a blind man with good eyes in his head, and a cripple with legs on. He sees two moons, and two doors to the public-house, and tries to find his way through both the doors at once. Over he goes, and there he must lie unless somebody will wheel him home in a barrow or carry him to the police-station.

Solomon says the glutton and the drunkard shall come to poverty, and that the drinker does in no time. He gets more and more down at the heel, and as his nose gets redder and his body is more swollen he gets to be more of a shack and more of a shark. His trade is gone, and his credit has run out, but he still manages to get his beer. He treats an old friend to a pot, and then finds that he has left his purse at home, and of course the old friend must pay the shot. He borrows till no one will lend him a groat, unless it is to get off lending a shilling. Shame has long since left him, though all who know him are ashamed of him. His talk runs like the tap, and is full of stale dregs: he is very kind over his beer, and swears he loves you, and would like to drink your health, and love you again. Poor sot, much good will his blessing do to any one who gets it; his poor wife and family have had too much of it already, and quake at the very sound of his voice.

Now, if we try to do anything to shut up a boozing-house, or shorten the hours for guzzling, we are called all sorts of bad names, and the wind-up of it all is—"What! Rob a poor man of his beer?" The fact is that they rob the poor man *by* his beer. The ale-jug robs the cupboard and the table, starves the wife and strips the children; it is a great thief, housebreaker, and heart-breaker, and the best possible thing is to break it to pieces, or keep it on the shelf bottom upwards. In a newspaper which was lent me the other day I saw some verses by John Barleycorn, jun., and as they tickled my fancy I copied them out, and here they are.

What! rob a poor man of his beer,
    And give him good victuals instead!
Your heart's very hard, sir, I fear,
    Or at least you are soft in the head.

What! rob a poor man of his mug,
    And give him a house of his own;
With kitchen and parlour so snug!
    'Tis enough to draw tears from a stone.

What! rob a poor man of his glass,
    And teach him to read and to write!
What! save him from being an ass!
    'Tis nothing but malice and spite.

What! rob a poor man of his ale,
    And prevent him from beating his wife,
From being locked up in jail,
    With penal employment for life!

What! rob a poor man of his beer,
    And keep him from starving his child!
It makes one feel awfully queer,
    And I'll thank you to draw it more mild.

Having given you a song, I now hand you a handbill to stick up in the "Rose and Crown" window, if the landlord wants an advertisement. It was written many years ago, but it is quite as good as new. Any beer-seller may print it who thinks it likely to help his trade.

DRUNKARDS, READ THIS!

DRUNKENNESS

EXPELS REASON
DISTEMPERS THE BODY,
DIMINISHES STRENGTH,
INFLAMES THE BLOOD;

CAUSES $\begin{Bmatrix} \text{INTERNAL} \\ \text{EXTERNAL} \\ \text{ETERNAL} \\ \text{INCURABLE} \end{Bmatrix}$ WOUNDS;

IS

A WITCH TO THE SENSES,
A DEMON TO THE SOUL,
A THIEF TO THE PURSE,
A GUIDE TO BEGGARY, LECHERY, & VILLAINY.

IT IS

THE WIFE'S WOE, AND
THE CHILDREN'S SORROW.

MAKES A MAN

WALLOW WORSE THAN A BEAST, AND
ACT LIKE A FOOL.

HE IS

A SELF-MURDERER;
WHO DRINKS TO ANOTHER'S GOOD HEALTH,

AND

ROBS HIMSELF OF HIS OWN.

EVERY MAN SHOULD SWEEP BEFORE HIS OWN DOOR

HE is a wise man who has wit enough for his own affairs. It is a common thing for people to *mind* Number One, but not so common to see people *mend* it. When it comes to spending money on labour or improvements, they think that repairs should begin at Number 2, and Number 3, and go on till all the houses up to Number 50 are touched up before any hint should be given to Number One. Now, this is very stupid, for if charity should begin at home, certainly reformation should begin there too. It is a waste of time to go far away to make a clearance, there's nothing like sweeping the snow from your own door. Let every dog carry his own tail. Mind your own business, and mend your own manners, and if every man does the same all will be minded and mended, as the old song says:

"Should every man defend his house,
    Then all would be defended;
If every man would mend a man,
    Then all mankind were mended."

A man who does not look well to his own concerns is not fit to be trusted with other people's. Lots of folks are so busy abroad that they have no time to look at home. They say the cobbler's wife goes barefoot, and the baker's child gets no buns, and the sweep's house has sooty chimneys. This comes of a man's thinking that he is everybody except himself. All the wit in the world is not in one head, and therefore the wisest man living is not bound to look after all his neighbour's matters. There are wonderful people about whose wisdom would beat Solomon into fits; and yet they have not sense enough to keep their own kettle from boiling over. They could manage the nation, and yet can't keep their boys out of the farmer's orchard; they could teach the parson, but they can't learn themselves. They poke their noses into other people's concerns, where they are as welcome as water in one's shoes, but as for setting their own house to rights, they like the job about as much as a pig likes having a ring put in his nose. The meddlesome man will not begin to darn his own stockings because he has left his needle sticking in his cousin's socks: he will be as grey as grannum's cat before he improves, and yet he struts like a crow in a gutter, and thinks himself cock of the walk.

A man's own selfishness and conceit ought to make him see to his own ways if nothing else does.

> There's but one wise man in the world,
>   And who d'ye think it be?
> 'Tis this man, that man, t'other man,
>   Every man thinks 'tis he.

Now, if this be so, why does not this wise man do the wise thing and set his own wise self in the way of growing wiser? Every cat cleans its own fur, and licks its own kittens: when will men and women mind their own minds, and busy themselves with their own business? Boil your own potatoes, and let me roast mine if I like; I won't do it with your firing. "Every man to his tent" was the old cry in Israel, and it's not a bad one for England, only Nelson gave us a better—

ENGLAND EXPECTS EVERY MAN TO DO HIS DUTY.

SCANT FEEDING OF MAN OR HORSE IS SMALL PROFIT AND SURE LOSS

WHAT is saved out of the food of cattle is a dead loss, for a horse can't work if he is not fed. If an animal won't pay for keeping he won't pay for starving. Even the land yields little if it is not nourished, and it is just the same with the poor beast. You might as well try to run a steam-engine without coals, or drive a watermill without water, as work a horse without putting corn into him. Thomas Tusser, who wrote a book upon "Husbandry" in the olden time, said,

> "Who starveth his cattle, and weareth them out
> By carting and ploughing, his gain I much doubt:
> But he that in labour doth use them aright
> Has gain to his comfort, and cattle in plight."

Poor dumb animals cannot speak for themselves, and therefore every one who has his speech should plead for them. To keep them short of victuals is a crying shame. I hate cruelty, and above all things the cruelty which starves the labouring beast.

> "A right good man is good to all,
> And stints not table, rack, or stall;
> Not only cares for horse and hog,
> But kindly thinks of cat and dog."

Is not a man better than a beast? Then, depend upon it, what is good for the ploughing horse is good for the ploughing boy: a belly full of plain food is a wonderful help to a labouring man. A starving workman is a dear servant. If you don't pay your men, they pay themselves, or else they shirk their work. He who labours well should be fed well, especially a ploughman.

> "Let such have enow
> That follow the plough."

There would be no bread if it were not for the ploughman: would you starve the man who is the very bottom and beginning of everything? John never brags, but he thinks well of his calling, and thinks well of those who pay well: as for those who grind the faces of the poor, the more John thinks of them the less he thinks of them. A man may live upon little, but Farmer Gripper thinks we can live upon nothing, which is a horse of another colour. I can't make out why the land cannot afford to keep those who work on it, for it used to do so. Tom Tusser wrote three hundred years ago,

> "Good ploughmen look weekly, of custom and right,
> For roast meat on Sundays, and Thursdays at night.
> Thus doing and keeping such custom and guise,
> They call thee good huswife, they love thee likewise."

This is what he writes to the farmer's wife about the ploughmen who lived at the farm house, but he has a bit to say for the other fellows and their privileges. About the harvest supper he says,

> "In harvest time, harvest folk, servants, and all,
> Should make altogether good cheer in the hall."

I wish they would, but then they are so apt to drink.
Could we not have a feast without the beer and the
headaches? This is old Tom's writing about the harvest
supper, and so on:

"For all this good feasting, yet art thou not loose,
Till ploughman thou givest his harvest home goose.
Though goose go in stubble, I pass not for that,
Let Giles have a goose, be she lean, be she fat."

I fancy I see old Gripper giving Giles a goose: he
would think Giles a green goose if he were to hint at it.
Gripper is a close shaver; where he grazes no goose
could pick up a living after him. He does not know
what his lean labourers say of him, but he might guess,
for a hungry man is an angry man, and an empty
belly makes no compliments. As for lazy fellows who
will eat till they sweat and work till they freeze, I
don't mind what short commons they get; but a real
hard-working man ought to be able to get for a day's
work enough to keep himself and family from hunger.
If this cannot be done, something is wrong somewhere,
as the man said when he sat down on a setting of eggs.
I am not going to blame the farmers, or the landlords,
or the Parliament men, or anybody; but the land is
good, and yields plenty for man and beast, and neither
horse nor man should be starved.

There is no gain in being niggardly to your cattle.
I have known men buy old screws of horses and feed
them badly, and yet pay more in the long run for
ploughing than the owner of a good team who gave out
a fair allowance. The poor things can't work if they
don't eat. As I said before, I speak up for the horses

because they can't speak for themselves. All they *can*
say, however, goes to prove what I have written: ask
them if they can plough well when they get bad corn,
and little of it, and they answer with a neigh.

As for the men, I wish they were, all round, a more
deserving set, but I am obliged to own that a many are
better at grubbing than ploughing. I would say to
them, "Do good work, and then ask for good
wages." I am afraid that many are not worth more
than they get. Our old master used to say to Crawley
Jones—

> "You feed so fast, and walk so very slow—
>   Eat with your legs, and with your grinders go."

But then, if Jones was a slow man, he certainly had slow
pay. He did not see the fun of working to the tune of
twenty shillings when he had only ten. If he had done
more master would have given him more, but Jones
couldn't see that, and so he mouched about, doing
next to nothing, and got next to nothing for it. He very
seldom got a bit of meat, and there was no bone or
muscle in the man. He seemed go be fed on turnip-
tops, and was as dull as a dormouse in winter time, and
unless you had emptied a skip of bees over him you
couldn't have woke him up. They say that Johnny
Raw is a stupid; he would not be half so stupid if he
had more *raw* to put in his pot.

> Though lubbers might loiter with belly too full,
> We're not in that case, but our belts we must pull;
> Could we manage to get a little more meat,
> We could do twice as much, and think it no feat.

They call a ploughman Chaw-bacon, do they? Wouldn't he like a bit more bacon to chaw? Hundreds and thousands of hard-working men down in the shires hardly get enough fat to grease the wheels of life, and the more's the pity. As to the poor women and children, it is often short-cake with them: bread, and pull it, and little of that.

One thing, however, is as plain as a pike-staff: the labourer cannot afford to keep a public house going while he has so little for his own private house. He has not a penny to spare, I'm sure but had need to take all home to the missus that he can make by hook or by crook. Miss Hannah More wrote two verses which every ploughman should read and mark, and learn.

> "We say the times are grievous hard,
>   And hard they are, 'tis true!
> But, drinkers, to your wives and babes
>   They're harder made by you.
>
> "The drunkard's tax is self-imposed,
>   Like every other sin;
> The taxes altogether cost
>   Not half so much as gin."

Well, if after all our being sober and thrifty, we cannot get along without pinching, let us still be patient and contented. We have more blessings than we can count even now. If masters happen to be close-fisted, God is open-handed, and if the outward food be scant, the bread of heaven is plentiful. Cheer up, brother ploughman, it's better on before. There is a city where "the very streets are paved with gold exceeding clear and fine." This should make us feel like singing all the time, and help us to follow the advice of old Thomas—

> "At bed, and at board, whatsoever befall,
> Whatever God sendeth, be merry withal."

NEVER STOP THE PLOUGH TO CATCH A MOUSE

THERE'S not much profit in this game. Think of a man and a boy and four horses all standing still for the sake of a mouse! What would old friend Tusser say to that? I think he would rhyme in this fashion—

> A ploughman deserveth a cut of the whip
> If for idle pretence he let the hours slip.

Heaps of people act like this. They have a great work in hand which wants all their wits, and they leave it to squabble over some pretty nothing, not worth a fig. Old master Tom would say to them—

> No more tittle tattle, go on with your cattle.

He could not bear for a farmer to let his horses out for carting even, because it took their work away from the farm, and so I am sure he would be in a great stew if he saw farmers wasting their time at matches, and hunts, and the like. He says—

> "Who slacketh his tillage a carter to be,
> For groat got abroad, at home shall lose three;
> For sure by so doing he brings out of heart,
> Both land for the corn, and horse for the cart."

The main chance must be minded, and the little things must be borne with. Nobody would burn his house down to kill the blackbeetles, and it would never answer to kill the bullocks to feed the cats. If our baker left off making bread for a week while he cracked the cockroaches, what should we all do for breakfast? If the butcher sold no more meat till he had killed all the blow-flies, we should be many a day without mutton. If the water companies never gave the Londoners a drink till they had fished every gudgeon out of the Thames, how would the old ladies make their tea? There's no use in stopping your fishing because of the sea-weed, nor your riding because of the dust.

Now, our minister said to me the other day, "John, if you were on the committees of some of our societies you would see this mouse-hunting done to perfection. Not only committees, but whole bodies of Christian people, go mouse-hunting." Well, said I, minister, just write me a bit, and I will stick it in my book, it will be beef to my horse-radish. Here's his writing:—

"A society of good Christian people will split into pieces over a petty quarrel, or mere matter of opinion, while all around them the masses are perishing for want of the gospel. A miserable little mouse, which no cat would ever hunt, takes them off from their Lord's work. Again, intelligent men will spend months of time and heaps of money in inventing and publishing mere speculations, while the great field of the world lies unploughed. They seem to care nothing how many may perish so long as they can ride their hobbies. In other matters a little common sense is allowed to rule, but in the weightiest matters foolishness is sadly conspicuous. As for you and me, John, let us kill a mouse when it nibbles our bread, but let us not spend our lives

over it. What can be done by a mousetrap or a cat
should not occupy all our thoughts.

The paltry trifles of this world are much of the same
sort. Let us give our chief attention to the chief things,
—the glory of God, the winning of souls for Jesus, and
our own salvation. There are fools enough in the world,
and there can be no need that Christian men should
swell the number. Go on with your ploughing, John,
and I will go on with my preaching, and in due season
we shall reap if we faint not."

A LOOKING GLASS IS OF NO USE TO A BLIND MAN

H E who will not see is much the same as if he had no eyes; indeed, in some things, the man without eyes has the advantage, for he is in the dark *and knows it*. A lantern is of no use to a bat, and good teaching is lost on the man who will not learn. Reason is folly with the unreasonable. One man can lead a horse to the water, but a hundred cannot make him drink: it is easy work to tell a man the truth, but if he will not be convinced your labour is lost. We pity the poor blind, we cannot do so much as that for those who shut their eyes against the light.

A man who is blind to his own faults is blind to his own interests. He who thinks that he never was a fool is a fool now. He who never owns that he is wrong will never get right. He'll mend, as the saying is, when he grows better, like sour beer in summer. How can a man take the smuts off his face if he will not look in the glass, nor believe that they are there when he is told of them?

Prejudice shuts up many eyes in total darkness. The man who knows already: he is positive and can swear to it, and it's no use your arguing. He has made up his mind, and it did not take him long, for there's very little of it, but when he has said a thing he sticks to it like cobbler's wax. He is wiser than seven men that can render a reason. He is as positive as if he had been on the other side of the curtain and looked into the back yard of the universe. He talks as if he carried all knowledge in his waistcoat pocket, like a peppermint lozenge. Those who like may try to teach him, but I don't care to hold up a mirror to a mole.

Some men are blinded by their worldly business, and could not see heaven itself if the windows were open over their heads. Look at farmer Grab, he is like Nebuchadnezzar, for his conversation is all among beasts, and if he does not eat grass it is because he never could stomach salads. His dinner is his best devotion, he is a terrible fastener on a piece of beef, and sweats at it more than at his labour. As old Master Earle says, "His religion is a part of his copyhold, which he takes from his landlord, and refers wholly to his lordship's discretion. If he gives him leave, he goes to church in his best clothes, and sits there with his neighbours, but never prays more than two prayers—for rain and for fair weather, as the case may be. He is a niggard all the week, except on market days, where, if his corn sell well, he thinks he may be drunk with a good conscience. He is sensible of no calamity but the burning of a stack of corn, or the overflowing of a meadow, and he thinks Noah's flood the greatest plague that ever was, not because it drowned the world, but spoiled the grass. For death he is never troubled, and if he gets in his harvest before it happens, it may come when it will, he cares not." He is as stubborn as he is stupid, and to get a new thought into his head you would need to bore a hole in his skull with a centre-bit. The game would not be worth the candle. We must leave him alone, for he is too old in the tooth, and too blind to be made to see.

Other people hurt their eyes by using glasses which are not spectacles. I have tried to convince Joe Scroggs that it would be a fine thing for him to join the tee-totallers, and he has nothing to say against it only "he does not see it."

> "He up and told me to my face,
>   The chimney corner should be his place,
>   And there he'd sit and dye his face,
>   And drink till all is blue."

All is blue with him now, for his furniture is nearly all sold, and his wife and children have not a shoe to their foot, and yet he laughs about "a yard of pump water," and tells me to go and drink my cocoa. Poor soul! Poor soul!

> In tippling is his sole delight,
>   Each sign-post bars his way;
> He spends in muddy ale at night
>   The wages of the day.

Can nothing be done for such poor fools? Why not shorten the hours for dealing out the drink? Why not shut up the public-houses on Sundays? If these people have not got sense enough to take care of themselves the law should protect them. Will Shepherd says he has to fetch his sheep out of a field when they are likely to get blown through eating too much green meat, and there ought to be power to fetch sots out of a beershop when they are worse than blowed through drink. How I wish I could make poor Scroggs see as I do, but there, if a fellow has no eyes he can't see the sun, though his nose is being scorched off in the glare of it.

Of all dust the worst for the eyes is gold dust. A bribe blinds the judgment, and riches darken the mind. As smoke to the eyes, so also is flattery to the soul, and prejudice turns the light of the sun into a darkness that may be felt. We are all blind by nature, and till the good Physician opens our eyes we grope, even in gospel light. All the preaching in the world cannot make a man see the truth so long as his eyes are blinded. There is a heavenly eye-salve which is a sovereign cure, but the worst of the matter is that the blind in heart think they see already, and so they are likely to die in darkness. Let us pray for those who never pray for themselves: God's power can do for them what is far beyond our power.

A dark and blinded thing is man,
    Yet full of fancied light!
But all his penetration can
    Obtain no gospel light.

Though heavenly truth may blaze abroad
    He cannot see at all;
Though gospel leaders show the road,
    He still gropes for the wall.

Perhaps he stands to hear the sound,
    But blind he still remains,
No meaning in the word is found
    To cause him joys or pains.

O Lord, thy holy power display,
    For thou the help must find;
Pour in the light of gospel day,
    Illuminate the blind.

Behold, how unconcerned they dwell
   Though reft of sight they be,
They fancy they can see right well.
   And need not help from thee.

Speak, and they'll mourn their blinded eyes,
   And cry to thee for light;
O Lord, do not our prayer despise,
   But give these blind men sight.

HE HAS GOT THE FIDDLE, BUT NOT THE STICK

IT often comes to pass that a man steps into another's shoes, and yet cannot walk in them. A poor tool of a parson gets into a good man's pulpit, and takes the same texts, but the sermons are chalk, and not cheese. A half-baked young swell inherits his father's money but not his generosity, his barns but not his brains, his title but not his sense—he has the fiddle without the stick, and the more's the pity.

Some people imagine that they have only to get hold of the plough-handles, and they would soon beat John Ploughman. If they had his fiddle they are sure they could play on it. J. P. presents his compliments, and wishes he may be there when it is done.

> "That I fain would see,
>   Quoth blind George of Hollowee."

However, between you and me and the bedpost, there is one secret which John does not mind letting out. John's fiddle is poor enough, but the stick is a right good one, too good to be called a fiddle-stick. Do you want to see the stick with which John plays his fiddle? Here it is—Looking to God for help, John always tries to do his best, whatever he has to do, and he has found this to be the very best way to play all kinds of tunes. What little music there is in John's poor old

fiddle comes out of it in that way. Listen to a scrape
or two.

> If I were a cobbler, I'd make it my pride
>   The best of all cobblers to be;
> If I were a tinker, no tinker beside
>   Should mend an old kettle like me.
>
> And being a ploughman, I plough with the best,
>   No furrow runs straighter than mine;
> I waste not a moment, and stay not to rest,
>   Though idlers to tempt me combine.
>
> Yet I wish not to boast, for trust I have none
>   In aught I can do or can be;
> I rest in my Saviour, and what he has done
>   To ransom poor sinners like me.

"GREAT CRY AND LITTLE WOOL," AS THE MAN SAID WHO CLIPPED THE SOW

OUR friend Hodge does not seem to be making much of an out at shearing. It will take him all his time to get wool enough for a blanket, and his neighbours are telling him so, but he does not heed them, for a man never listens to reason when he has made up his mind to act unreasonably. Hodge gets plenty of music of a sort: Hullah's system is nothing to it, and even Nebuchadnezzar's flutes, harps, sackbuts and dulcimers could not make more din. He gets "cry" enough to stock a Babylon of babies, but not wool enough to stop his ears with.

Now, is not this very like the world with its notions of pleasure? There is noise enough; laughter and shouting, and boasting; but where is the comfort which can warm the heart and give peace to the spirit? Generally there's plenty of smoke and very little fire in what is called pleasure. It promises a nag and gives an egg. Gaiety is a sort of flash in the pan, a fifth of November squib, all fizz and bang and done for. The devil's meal is all bran, and the world's wine turns to vinegar. It is always making a great noise over nutshells. Thousands have had to weep over their blunder in looking for their heaven on earth; but they follow each other like sheep through a gap, not a bit the wiser for the experience of generations. It seems that every man must have a clip at his own particular pig, and cannot be made to believe that like all the rest it will yield him nothing but bristles. Men are not all of one mind as to what is best for them; they no more agree than the clocks in our village, but they all hang together in following after vanity, for to the core of their hearts they are vain.

One shears the publican's hog, which is so fond of the swill tub, and he reckons upon bringing home a wonderful lot of wool; but everybody knows that he who goes to the "Woolpack" for wool will come home shorn: the "Blue Boar" is an uncommonly ugly animal to shear, and so is the "Red Lion." Better sheer off as fast as you can; it will be sheer folly to stop. You may loaf about the tap of the "Halfmoon" till you get the full moon in your noddle, and need a keeper: it is the place for men whose wits go woolgathering, but wool there is none.

Another is covetous, and hopes to escape misery by being a miser: his greedy mind can no more be filled than a lawyer's purse: he never has enough, and so he never has a feast. He makes money with his teeth, by keeping them idle. That is a very lean hog to clip at, for poverty wants some things, luxury many things, but covetousness wants all things. If we could hoard up all the money in the world, what would it be to us at last? To-day at good cheer, to-morrow on the bier: in the midst of life we are in death.

Some, like old Mrs. Too-good, go in for self-righteousness, and their own mouths dub them saints. They are the pink of perfection, the cream of creation, the gems of their generation, and yet a sensible man would not live in the same house with them for all the money you could count. They are saints abroad, but ask their maids what they are at home. Great cry and little wool is common enough in religion: you will find that those who crack themselves up are generally cracked, and those who despise their neighbours come to be despised themselves.

Many try wickedness, and run into bad company, and rake the kennels of vice. I warrant you they may shear the whole styful of filthy creatures and never find a morsel of wool on the whole lot of them. Loose characters, silly amusements, gambling, wantonness, and such like, are swine that none but a fool will try his shears upon. I don't deny that there's plenty of swinish music—who ever expected that there would be silence in a piggery? But then noise cannot fill the heart, nor laughter lighten the soul.

John Ploughman has tried for himself, and he knows by experience that all the world is nothing but a hog that is not worth the shearing: "Vanity of vanities, all is vanity." But yet there is wool to be had; there are real joys to be got for the asking if we ask aright. Below, all things deceive us, but above us there is a true Friend. "Wherefore do ye spend your money for that which is not bread, and your labour for that which satisfieth not?" This is John Ploughman's verdict, which he wishes all his readers to take note of—

> "Faith in Jesus Christ will give
> Sweetest pleasures while we live;
> Faith in Jesus must supply
> Solid comfort when we die."

YOU MAY BEND THE SAPLING, BUT
NOT THE TREE

LADDER, and pole, and cord will be of no use to
straighten the bent tree; it should have been
looked after much earlier. Train trees when they
are saplings and young lads before the down comes
on their chins. If you want a bullfinch to pipe, whistle
to him while he is young; he will scarcely catch the
tune after he has learnt the wild bird's note. Begin
early to teach, for children begin early to sin. Catch
them young and you may hope to keep them.

> Ere your boy has reached to seven,
> Teach him well the way to heaven;
> Better still the work will thrive,
> If he learns before he's five.

What is learned young is learned for life. What we
hear at the first we remember to the last. The bent
twig grows up a crooked tree. Horse-breakers say

> "The tricks a colt getteth at his first backing,
> Will whilst he continueth never be lacking."

When a boy is rebellious, conquer him, and do it well
the first time, that there may be no need to do it again.
A child's first lesson should be obedience, and after
that you may teach it what you please: yet the young
mind must not be laced too tight, or you may hurt its
growth and hinder its strength. They say a daft nurse

makes a wise child, but I do not believe it: nobody needs so much common sense as a mother or a governess. It does not do to be always thwarting; and yet remember if you give a child his will and a whelp his fill, both will surely turn out ill. A child's back must be made to bend, but it must not be broken. He must be ruled, but not with a rod of iron. His spirit must be conquered, but not crushed.

Nature does sometimes overcome nurture, but for the most part the teacher wins the day. Children are what they are made: the pity is that so many are spoiled in the bringing up. A child may be rocked too hard; you may spoil him either by too much cuffing or too much kissing. I knew two boys who had a Christian mother, but she always let them have their own way. The consequence was that when they grew up they took to drinking and low company and soon spent the fortune their father left them. No one controlled them and they had no control over themselves, and so they just rattled along the broad road like butcher boys with runaway horses, and there was no stopping them. A birch or two worn out upon them when they were little would have been a good use of timber.

Still, a child can be treated too hardly, and especially he can be shut up too many hours in school, when a good run and a game of play would do him more good. Cows don't give any the more milk for being often milked, nor do children learn any more because of very long hours in a hot room.

A boy can be driven to learn till he loses half his wits: forced fruits have little flavour; a man at five is a fool at fifteen. If you make veal of the calf he will never turn to beef. Yet learning may be left so long that the little dunce is always behindhand.

There's a medium in everything and he is a good father who hits upon it, so that he governs his family with love, and his family loves to be governed by him. Some are like Eli, who let his sons sin and only chided them a little; these will turn out to be cruel parents in the long run: others are too strict, and make home miserable, and so drive the youngsters to the wrong road in another way. Tight clothes are very apt to tear, and hard laws are often broken: but loose garments tear too, and where there are no laws at all, things are sure to go amiss. So you see it is easy to err on either side, and hard to dance the tight-rope of wisdom. Depend on it, he who has a wife and bairns will never be short of care to carry. See what we get when we come to marry, yet many there are who will not tarry.

In these days children have a deal too much of their own way, and often make their mothers and fathers their slaves. It has come to a fine pass when the goslings teach the geese, and the kittens rule the cat: it is the upsetting of everything, and no parent ought to put up with it. It is as bad for the boys and girls as it is for the grown folk, and it brings out the worst side of their characters. I would sooner be a cat on hot bricks, or a toad under a harrow, than let my own children be my masters. No, the head must be the head, or it will hurt the whole body.

> For children out of place
> Are a father's disgrace,
> If you rule not you'll rue,
> For they'll quickly rule you.

A MAN MAY LOVE HIS HOUSE, THOUGH HE RIDE NOT ON THE RIDGE

YOU can love your house and not ride on the ridge; there's a medium in everything. You can be fond of your wife without being her drudge, and you can love your children dearly, and yet not give them their own way in everything. Some men are of so strange a kidney that they set no bounds to their nonsense. If they are fond of roast beef they must needs suck the spit; they cannot rest with eating the pudding, they must swallow the bag. If they dislike a thing, the very smell of it sets them grumbling, and if they like it they must have it everywhere and always, for nothing else is half so sweet. When they do go in for eating rabbits, they have

> Rabbits young and rabbits old,
> Rabbits hot and rabbits cold,
> Rabbits tender, rabbits tough:
> Never can they have enough.

Whatever they take up takes them up, and for a season they cannot seize on anything else. At election times the barber cannot trim his customer's poll because of the polling, and the draper cannot serve you with calico because he is canvassing. The nation would go to the dogs altogether if the cat's-meat man did not secure the election by sticking his mark on the ballot paper. It is supposed that the globe would leave off turning round if our Joe Scroggs did not go down to

the "Dun Cow", and read the paper, and have his say
upon politics, in the presence of the house of commons
assembled in the taproom. I do not quite think so, but
I know this, that when the Whigs and the Tories and
the Radicals are about, Scroggs is good for nothing all
day long. What party he belongs to I don't know, but I
believe his leading principle will be seen in the following verse:—

> If gentlemen propose a glass
>   He never says them nay;
> For he always thinks it right to drink
>   While other people pay.

You can make a good thing become a nuisance by
harping on that one string from dawn to dusk. A hen
with one chick makes no end of scratching and clucking,
and so does a fellow of one idea. He has a bee in his
bonnet, and he tries to put a wasp in yours. He duns
you, and if you do not agree with him he counts you
his enemy. When you meet with him you are unfortunate, and when you leave him you will better
yourself go where you may: "there's small sorrow at
our parting," as the old mare said to the broken cart.
You may try to humour him, but he will have all the
more humours if you do, for the man knows no modera-
tion, and if you let him ride on the roof he will soon
sit on the chimney-pot.

One man of my acquaintance used to take Morrison's
pills every day of his life, and when I called in to see
him I had not been there ten minutes before he wanted
me to take a dose, but I could not swallow what he told
me nor the pills either, so I told him I dare say they

were very good for him, but they did not suit my constitution: however, he kept on with his subject till I was fain to be off. Another man never catches sight of me but he talks about vaccination and goes on against it till he froths at the mouth, and I am half afraid he will inoculate me. My master had a capital horse, worth a good deal of money, only he always shied at a stone-heap on the road, and if there were fifty of them he always bolted off the road every time. He had got heaps on his brain, poor creature, and though he was fit for a nobleman's carriage he had to be put to plough. Some men have got stone-heaps in their poor noddles and this spoils them for life and makes it dangerous for all who have to deal with them. What queer fish there are in our pond! I am afraid that most of us have a crack somewhere, but we don't all show it quite so much as some. We ought to have a good deal of patience, and then we shall find amusement where else we should be bothered to death. One of my mates says the world is not round, and so I always drop into his notion and tell him this is a flat world and he is a flat too.

What a trial it is to be shut up for an hour with a man or a woman with a hobby; riding in a horse-box with a bear with a sore head is nothing to it. The man is so fond of bacon that he wants you to kiss his pig, and all the while you hope you will never again see either the man or his pork as long as you live. No matter what the whole hog may be, the man who goes it is terrible.

> Rocking horse for boy,
> Hobby horse for man:
> Each one rides his toy
> Whenever he can.

The boy is right glad
Though he rideth alone;
His father's own fad
By the world must be known.

Of the two hobby rides,
The boy's is the best;
For the man often chides,
And gives you no rest.

It is a good thing for a man to be fond of his own
trade and his own place, but still there is reason in
everything, even in roasting eggs. When a man thinks
that his place is below him he will pretty soon be below
his place, and therefore a good opinion of your own
calling is by no means an evil; yet nobody is everybody,
and no trade is to crow over the rest. The cobbler has
his awl but he is not all, and the hatter wears a crown
but he is not king. A man may come to market without
buying my onions, and ploughing can be done with
other horses than mine, though Dapper and Violet are
something to brag of. The farming interest is no doubt
first, and so is the saddler's, and so is the tinker's, and
so is the grocer's and so is the draper's, and so is the
parson's, and so is the parish beadle's, and so is every
other interest according to each man's talk.

Your trade, as a trade, is all very well,
But other good folk have their cheeses to sell;
You must not expect all the world to bow down,
And give to one pedlar the sceptre and crown.

It is astonishing how much men will cry up small
matters. They are very busy, but it is with catching

flies. They talk about a mushroom till you would think it was the only thing at the Lord Mayor's dinner, and the beef and the turkeys went for nothing. They say nothing about the leg of mutton, for they are so much in love with the trimmings. They can't keep things in their places, but make more of a horse's tail than they do of his whole body. Like the cock on the dunghill, they consider a poor barley-corn to be worth more than a diamond. A thing happens to suit their taste and so there is nothing like it in the whole of England; no, nor in all America or Australia. A duck will not always dabble in the same gutter, but they will; for, bless your heart, they don't think it a gutter, but a river, if not an ocean. They must ride the ridge of the roof, or else burn the house down. A good many people love their dogs, but these folks take them to bed with them. Other farmers fat the calf, but they fall down and worship it, and what is worse they quarrel with everybody who does not think as much of their idol as they do.

It will be a long while before all men become wise, but it will help on the time if we begin to be wise ourselves. Don't let us make too much of this world and the things of it. We are to use it but not to abuse it; to live *in* it but not *for* it; to love our house but not to ride on the ridge. Our daily bread and daily work are to be minded, and yet we must not mind earthly things. We must not let the body send the soul to grass, rather must we make the limbs servants to the soul. The world must not rule us, we must reign as kings though we are only ploughmen; and stand upright even if the world should be turned upside down.

GREAT DRINKERS THINK THEMSELVES GREAT MEN

WONDERFUL men and white rats are not so scarce as most people think. Folks may talk as they like about Mr. Gladstone and Lord Beaconsfield, and that sharp gentleman Bismarck, but Jack, and Tom, and Harry, and scores more that I know of, could manage their business for them a fine sight better; at least, they think so, and are quite ready to try. Great men are as plentiful as mice in an old wheat-stack down our way. Every parish has one or two wonderful men; indeed, most public-houses could show one at least, and generally two; and I have heard that on Saturday nights, when our "Blue Dragon" is full, there may be seen as many as twenty of the greatest men in all the world in the taproom, all making themselves greater by the help of pots of beer. When the jug has been filled and emptied a good many times, the black-smith feels he ought to be prime minister; Styles, the carter, sees the way to take off all the taxes, and Old Hob, the rat-catcher, roars out—

> "They're all a pack of fools,
> And good-for-nothing tools;
> If they'd only send for me,
> You'd see how things would be."

If you have a fancy to listen to these great men when they are talking you need not go into the bar, for you can hear them outside the house; they generally speak four or five at a time, and every one in a Mitcham whisper, which is very like a shout. What a fine flow of words they have! There's no end to it, and it's a pity there was ever any beginning, for there's generally a mix up of foul talk with their politics, and this sets them all roaring with laughter. A few evenings in such company would poison the mind of the best lad in the parish. I am happy to say that these great men have to be turned out at ten o'clock, for then our public-house closes; and none too soon, I'm sure.

A precious little is enough to make a man famous in certain companies; one fellow knocked a man's eye out at a prize-fight; another stowed away twice as much pudding as four pigs could have disposed of; another stood on his head and drank a glass of beer; and another won a prize by grinning through a horse-collar; and for such things as these the sots of the village think mightily of them. Little things please little minds, and nasty things please dirty minds. If I were one of these wonderful fellows I would ask the nearest way to a place where nobody would know me.

Now I am at it, I will notice a few other wonderful bodies who sometimes condescend to look down on a ploughman; but before I make them angry I would give them a verse from one of my old uncle's songs, which I have shaped a bit.

"I hope none will be offended with me for writing this,
For it is not intended for anything amiss;
If you consider kindly my remarks you will allow,
For what can you expect from one whose hand is on
the plough?"

I used to feel quite staggered when I heard of an amazing clever man, but I've got used to it, as the rook did to the scarecrow when he found out that it was a stuffed nothing. Like the picture which looked best at a very long distance off, so do most clever fellows. They are swans a mile off, but geese when you get near them. Some men are too knowing to be wise, their boiler bursts because they have more steam than they can use. They know too much, and having gone over the top of the ladder they have gone down on the other side. People who are really wise never think themselves so: one of them said to me the other day,—

> "All things I thought I knew; but now confess
> The more I know I know I know the less."

Simple Simon is in a sad plight in such a world as this, but on the whole he gets on better than a fellow who is too clever by half. Every mouse had need have its eyes open nowadays, for the cats are very many and uncommonly sharp; and yet, you mark my word, most of the mice that are caught are the knowing ones. Somehow or other, in an ordinary sort of a world like this, it does not answer to be so over and above clever. Those who are up to so many dodges, find the dodges come down on them before long. My neighbour Hinks was much too wise a man to follow the plough, like poor shallow-pated John Ploughman, and so he took to scheming, and has schemed himself into one of the largest mansions in the country, where he will be provided with oakum to pick and a crank to turn during the next six calendar months. He had better have been a fool, for his cleverness has cost him his character.

When a man is too clever to tell the truth he will bring himself into no end of trouble before long. When he is too clever to stick to his trade, he is like the dog that let the meat fall into the water through trying to catch at its shadow. Clever Jack can do everything and can do nothing. He intends to be rich all at once, and despises small gains, and therefore is likely to die a beggar. When puffing is trusted and honest trading is scoffed at, time will not take long to wind up the concern. Work is as needful now as ever it was if a man would thrive; catching birds by putting salt on their tails would be all very well, but the creatures will not hold their tails still, and so we had better catch them in the usual way. The greatest trick for getting on in business is to work hard and to live hard. There's no making bread without flour, nor building houses without labour. I know the old saying is—

> "No more mortar, no more brick,
> A cunning knave has a cunning trick;"

but for all that things go on much the same as ever, and bricks and mortar are still wanted.

I see in the papers, every now and then, that some of the clever gentlemen who blow up bubble companies are pulled up before the courts. Serve them right! May they go where my neighbour Hinks is, every one of them. How many a poor tradesman is over head and ears in difficulty through them! I hope in future all men will fight shy of these fine companies, and swell managers, and very clever men. Men are neither suddenly rich nor suddenly good. It is all a bag of moonshine when a man would persuade you that he

knows a way of earning money by winking your eye.
We have all heard of the scheme for making deal boards
out of sawdust, and getting butter out of mud, but we
mean to go on with the saw-mill, and keep on milking
the cows; for between you and me and the blind mare,
we have a notion that the plans of idiots and very
clever men are as like as two peas in a shell.

The worst sort of clever men are those who know
better than the Bible and are so learned that they
believe that the world had no Maker, and that men
are only monkeys with their tails rubbed off. Dear, dear
me, this is the sort of talk we used to expect from Tom
of Bedlam, but now we get it from clever men. If things
go on in this fashion a poor ploughman will not be
able to tell which is the lunatic and which is the philoso-
pher. As for me, the old Book seems to be a deal easier
to believe than the new notions, and I mean to keep
to it. Many a drop of good broth is made in an old pot,
and many a sweet comfort comes out of the old doctrine.
Many a dog has died since I first opened my eyes, and
every one of these dogs has had his day, but in all the
days put together they have never hunted out a real
fault in the Bible, nor started anything better in its
place. They may be very clever, but they will not find a
surer truth than that which God teaches, nor a better
salvation than that which Jesus brings, and so finding
my very life in the gospel I mean to live in it, and so
ends this chapter.

TWO DOGS FIGHT FOR A BONE, AND A THIRD RUNS AWAY WITH IT

WE have all heard of the two men who quarrelled over an oyster, and called in a judge to settle the question: he ate the oyster himself, and gave them a shell each. This reminds me of the story of the cow which two farmers could not agree about, and so the lawyers stepped in and milked the cow for them, and charged them for their trouble in drinking the milk. Little is got by law, but much is lost by it. A suit in law may last longer than any suit a tailor can make you, and you may yourself be worn out before it comes to an end. It is better far to make matters up and keep out of court, for if you are caught there you are caught in the brambles, and won't get out without damage. John Ploughman feels a cold sweat at the thought of getting into the hands of lawyers. He does not mind going to Jericho, but he dreads the gentlemen on the road, for they seldom leave a feather upon any goose which they pick up.

However, if men will fight they must not blame the lawyers; if law were cheaper, quarrelsome people would have more of it, and quite as much would be spent in the long run. Sometimes, however, we get dragged into court willy nilly, and then one had need be wise as a serpent and harmless as a dove. Happy is he who finds an honest lawyer, and does not try to be his own client. A good lawyer always tries to keep

" Two dogs fight for a bone "

people out of law; but some clients are like moths with the candle, they must and will burn themselves. He who is so wise that he cannot be taught will have to pay for his pride.

> Let dogs delight to bark and bite;
>   And lose the marrow bone;
> Let bears and lions growl and fight,
>   I'll let the law alone.
>
> To suffer wrong is surely sad,
>   But law-suits are in vain;
> To throw good money after bad
>   Will but increase my pain.

HE LIVES UNDER THE SIGN OF THE CAT'S FOOT

THE question was once asked, When should a man marry? and the merry answer was, that for young men it is too soon and for old men it is too late. This is all very fine, but it will not wash. Both the wisdom and the folly of men seem banded together to make a mock of this doctrine. Men are such fools that they must and will marry even if they marry fools. It is wise to marry when we can marry wisely, and then the sooner the better. How many show their sense in choosing a partner it is not for me to say, but I fear that in many cases love is blind, and makes a very blind choice. I don't suppose that some people would ever get married at all if love had its wits about it. It is a mystery how certain parties ever found partners; truly there's no accounting for tastes. However, as they make their bed they must lie on it, and as they tie the knot they must be tied by it. If a man catches a tartar, or lets a tartar catch him, he must take his dose of tartaric acid, and make as few ugly faces as he can. If a three-legged stool come flying through the air, he must be thankful for such a plain token of love from the woman of his choice, and the best thing he can do is to sit down on it, and wait for the next little article.

When it is said of a man, "He lives under the sign of the cat's foot," he must try and please his pussy that she may not scratch him more than such cats generally do. A good husband will generally have a good wife, or make a bad wife better. Bad Jack makes a great noise about bad Jill, but there's generally twenty of one where there's a score of the other. They say a burden of one's own choosing is never felt to be heavy, but I don't know, some men are loaded with mischief as soon as they have a wife to carry. Yet

> A good woman is worth, if she were sold,
> The fairest crown that's made of gold.

She is a pleasure, a treasure, and a joy without measure. A good wife and health are a man's best wealth; and he who is in such a case should envy no man's place. Even when a woman is a little tart it is better than if she had no spirit, and made her house into a dirt pie. A shrew is better than a slut, though one can be quite miserable enough with either. If she is a good housewife, and looks well after the children, one may put up with a Caudle lecture now and then, though a cordial lecture would be a deal better. A husband is in a pickle indeed if he gets tied up to a regular scold; he might as well be skinned and set up to his neck in a tub of brine. Did you ever hear the scold's song? Read it, you young folks who think of committing matrimony, and think twice before you get married once.

> When in the morn I ope mine eyes
>   To entertain the day,
> Before my husband e'en can rise,
>   I scold him—then I pray.

When I at table take my place,
　　Whatever be the meat,
I first do scold—and then say grace,
　　If so disposed to eat.

Too fat, too lean, too hot, too cold,
　　I always do complain;
Too raw, too roast, too young, too old—
　　Faults I will find or feign.

Let it be flesh, or fowl, or fish,
　　It never shall be said,
But I'll find fault with meat or dish,
　　With master, or with maid.

But when I go to bed at night
　　I heartily do weep,
That I must part with my delight—
　　I cannot scold and sleep.

However, this doth mitigate
　　And much abate my sorrow,
That though to-night it be too late,
　　I'll early scold to-morrow.

When the husband is not a man it is not to be wondered at if the wife wears the top-boots: the mare may well be the best horse when the other horse is a donkey. Well may a woman feel that she is lord and master when she has to earn the living for the family, as is sometimes the case. She ought not to be the head, but if she has all the brains, what is she to do? What poor dawdles many men would be without their wives! As poor softy Simpkins says, if Bill's wife becomes a widow who will cut the pudding up for him, and will there be a pudding at all? It is grand when the wife knows her place, and keeps it, and they both pull together in everything. Then she is a helpmeet indeed and makes the house a home. Old friend Tusser says,

> "When husband is absent let housewife be chief,
> And look to their labour who live from their sheaf,
> The housewife's so named for she keepeth the house,
> And must tend on her profit as cat on a mouse."

He is very pat upon it that much of household affairs must rest on the wife, and he writes,—

> "Both out, not allow,
> Keep home, housewife thou."

Like the old man and woman in the toy which shows the weather, one must be sure to be in if the other goes out. When the king is abroad the queen must reign at home, and when he returns to his throne he is bound to look upon her as his crown, and prize her above gold and jewels. He should feel "if there's only one good wife in the whole world, I've got her." John Ploughman has long thought just that of his own wife, and after five-and-twenty years he is more sure of it than ever. He never bets, but he would not mind wagering a farthing cake that there is not a better woman on the surface of the globe than his own, very own beloved. Happy is the man who is happy in his wife. Let him love her as he loves himself, and a little better, for she is his better half.

> Thank God that hath so blest thee
> And sit down, John, and rest thee.

There is one case in which I don't wonder if the wife does put her mate under the cat's foot, and that is when he slinks off to the public, and wastes his wages. Even then love and gentleness is the best way of getting him home; but, really, some topers have no feeling, and laugh at kindness, and therefore nobody can be surprised if the poor wife bristles up and gives her lord and master a taste of tongue. Nothing tries married love more than the pot-house. Wages wasted, wife neglected, children in rags: if she gives it him hot and strong who can blame her? Pitch into him, good woman, and make him ashamed of himself, if you can. No wonder that you lead a cat and dog life while he is such a sorry dog.

Still, you may as well go home and set him a better example, for two blacks will never make a white, and if you put him in hot water he's sure to get some spirits to mix with it.

HE WOULD PUT HIS FINGER IN THE PIE, AND SO HE BURNT HIS NAIL OFF

SOME men must have a finger in every pie, or, as the proverb hath it, "their oar must be in every man's boat." They seem to have no business except to poke their noses into other people's business: they ought to have snub noses, for they are pretty sure to be snubbed. Prying and spying, peddling and meddling, these folks are in everybody's way, like the old toll-gate. They come without being sent for, stop without being asked, and cannot be got rid of, unless you take them by the left leg and throw them down stairs, and if you do that they will limp up again, and hope they don't intrude. No one pays them, and yet they give advice more often than any lawyer; and though no one ever thanks them, yet there they are, peeping through keyholes and listening under the eaves. They are as great at asking questions as if they wanted you to say the catechism, and as eager to give their opinion as if you had gone down on your knees to ask it.

These folks are like dogs that fetch and carry; they run all over the place like starlings when they are feeding their young. They make much ado, but never do much, unless it is mischief, and at this they are as apt as jackdaws. If any man has such people for his acquaintances, he may well say, "save me from my friends."

> I know your assistance you'll lend,
> When I want it I'll speedily send;
> You need not be making such stir,
> But mind your own business, good sir.

It is of no more use than if we spoke to the pigs, for here is Paul Pry again. Paul and his cousins are most offensive people, but you cannot offend them if you try.

Well do I remember the words of a wise old Quaker:—"John," said he, "be not concerned with that which concerns not thee." This taught me a lesson, and I made up my mind not to scrub other people's pigs for fear I should soon want scrubbing myself. There is a woman in our village who finds fault with all, and all find fault with her; they say her teeth are all loose through her tongue rubbing against them; if she could but hold her tongue she would be happy enough, but that's the difficulty—

> "When hens fall a cackling take heed to the nest,
> When drabs fall a whispering farewell to thy rest."

Will Shepherd was sitting very quiet while others were running down their neighbours. At last a loose fellow sung out "Look at old Will, he is as silent as a stock-fish; is it because he is wise or because he is a fool?" "Well," said Will, "you may settle that question how you like, but I have been told that a fool cannot be silent." Will is set down as very odd, but he is generally even with them before he has done. One thing is sure, he cares very little what they do say so long as they don't worry his sheep. He hummed in my

ear an old-fashioned verse or two the other evening,
omething like this—

> "Since folks will judge me every day,
> Let every man his judgment say;
> I will take it all as children's play,
> For I am as I am, whoever say nay.
>
> Many there be that take delight
> To judge a man's ways in envy and spite;
> But whether they judge me wrong or right,
> I am as I am, and so do I write.
>
> How the truth is I leave to you;
> Judge as ye list, whether false or true.
> Ye know no more than before ye knew,
> For I am as I am whatever ensue."

If folks will meddle with our business it is best to
ake no notice of them; there's no putting them out
ike letting them stop where they are; they are never so
ffended as when people neither offend them nor take
ffence at them. You might as soon stop all the frogs
rom croaking as quiet idle gossips when they once get
n the chat. Stuff your ear with wool and let them
abber till their tongue lies still, because they have
worn all the skin off it. "Where no wood is the fire
oeth out," and if you don't answer them they can't
nake a blaze for want of fuel. Treat them kindly, but
on't give them the treat of quarrelling with them.
ollow peace with all men, even if you cannot overtake
t.

YOU CAN'T CATCH THE WIND IN
A NET

SOME people get windmills in their heads, and go
in for all sorts of silly things. They talk of ruling
the nation as if men were to be driven like sheep,
and they prate of reforms and systems as if they could
cut out a world in brown paper, with a pair of scissors.
Such a body thinks himself very deep, but he is as
shallow as a milk-pan. You can soon know him as well
as if you had gone through him with a lighted candle,
and yet you will not know a great deal after all. He has
a great head, and very little in it. He can talk by the
dozen, or the gross, and say nothing. When he is
fussing and boasting of his fine doings you soon dis-
cover that he makes a long harvest of very little corn.
His tongue is like a pig's tail, going all day long and
nothing done.

This is the man who can pay off the National Debt,
and yet, in his little shop, he sells two apples in three
days: he has the secret of high farming, and loses more
at it than any man in the county. The more he studies
the more he misses the mark; he reminds me of a blind
man on a blind horse, who rode out in the middle of a
dark night, and the more he tried to keep out of ditches
the more he fell in.

When they catch live red herrings on Newmarket
heath he will bring out a good thing, and line his
pockets with gold; up till now, he says, he has been

unlucky, and he believes that if he were to make a man a coffin he would be sure not to die. He is going to be rich next year, and you will then see what you shall see: just now he would be glad of half a crown on account, for which he will give you a share in his invention for growing wheat without ploughing or sowing.

It is odd to see this wise man at times when his wits are all up in the moon: he is just like Chang, the Chinaman, who said, "Here's my umbrella, and here's my bundle, but *where am I*?" He cannot find his spectacles though he is looking through them; and when he is out riding on his own ass, he pulls up and says, "Wherever is that donkey?"

I have heard of one learned man who boiled his watch and stood looking at the egg, and another who forgot that he was to be married that day, and would have lost his lady if his friend had not fetched him out of his study. Think of that, my boy, and don't fret yourself because you are not so overdone with learning as to have forgotten your common sense.

The regular wind-catcher is soft as silk and as green as grass, and yet he thinks himself very long-headed; and so indeed he would be if his ears were taken into the measurement. He is going to do—well—there's no telling what. He is full of wishes but short of will, and so his buds never come to flowers or fruit. He is like a hen that lays eggs, and never sits on them long enough to hatch a single chick.

Moonshine is the article our friend deals in, and it is wonderful what he can see by it. He cries up his schemes, and it is said that he draws on his imagination for his facts. When he is in full swing with one of his notions, he does not stick at a trifle. Will Shepherd heard one of these gentry the other day telling how his new company would lead all the shareholders on to Tom Tiddler's ground to pick up gold and silver; and when all the talk was over, Will said to me, "That's a lie, with a lid on, and a brass handle to take hold of it." Rather sharp this of Will, for I do believe the man was caught on his own hook and believed in his own dreams; yet I did not like him, for he wanted us poor fellows to put our little savings into his hands, as if we could afford to fly kites with labourers' wages.

What a many good people there are who have religious crazes! They do nothing, but they have wonderful plans for doing everything in a jiffy. So many thousand people are to give half a crown each, and so many more a crown, and so many more a sovereign, and the meeting-house is to be built just so, and no how else. The mischief is that the thousands of people do not rush forward with their money, and the minister and a few hard-working friends have to get it together little by little in the old-fashioned style, while your wonderful schemer slinks out of the way and gives nothing. I have long ago found out that pretty things on paper had better be kept there. Our master's eldest son had a plan for growing plum-trees in our hedges as they do in Kent, but he never looked to see whether the soil would suit, and so he lost the trees which he put in, and there was an end of his damsons.

> "Circumstances alter cases;
> Different ways suit different places."

New brooms sweep clean, but they mostly sweep up dirt. Plough with what you please, I stick to the old horses which have served me so well. Fine schemes come to nothing; it is hard work that does it, whether it be in the world or in the church.

> "In the laborious husbandman you see
>   What all true Christians are or ought to be."

BEWARE OF THE DOG

JOHN PLOUGHMAN did not in his first book weary his friends by preaching, but in this one he makes bold to try his hand at a sermon, and hopes he will be excused if it should prove to be only a ploughman's preachment.

If this were a regular sermon preached from a pulpit of course I should make it long and dismal, like a winter's night, for fear people should call me eccentric. As it is only meant to be read at home, I will make it short, though it will not be sweet, for I have not a sweet subject. The text is one which has a great deal of meaning in it, and is to be read on many a wall. "BEWARE OF THE DOG." You know what dogs are, and you know how you beware of them when a bull-dog flies at you to the full length of his chain; so the words don't want any clearing up.

It is very odd that the Bible never says a good word for dogs: I suppose the breed must have been bad in those eastern parts, or else, as our minister tells me, they were nearly wild, had no master in particular, and were left to prowl about half starved. No doubt a dog is very like a man, and becomes a sad dog when he has himself for a master. We are all the better for having somebody to look up to; and those who say they care for nobody and nobody cares for them are dogs of the worst breed, and, for a certain reason, are never likely to be drowned.

Dear friends, I shall have heads and tails like other parsons, and I am sure I have a right to them, for they are found in the subjects before us.

Firstly, let us *beware of a dirty dog*—or as the grand old Book calls them, "evil workers"—those who love filth and roll in it. Dirty dogs will spoil your clothes, and make you as foul as themselves. A man is known by his company; if you go with loose fellows your character will be tarred with the same brush as theirs. People can't be very nice in their distinctions; if they see a bird always flying with the crows, and feeding and nesting with them, they call it a crow, and ninety-nine times out of a hundred they are right. If you are fond of the kennel, and like to run with the hounds, you will never make the world believe that you are a pet lamb. Besides, bad company does a man real harm, for, as the old proverb has it, if you lie down with dogs you will get up with fleas.

You cannot keep too far off a man with the fever and a man of wicked life. If a lady in a fine dress sees a big dog come out of a horse-pond, and run about shaking himself dry, she is very particular to keep out of his way, and from this we may learn a lesson,—when we see a man half gone in liquor, sprinkling his dirty talk all around him, our best place is half a mile off at the least.

Secondly, *beware of all snarling dogs*. There are plenty of these about; they are generally very small creatures, but they more than make up for their size by their noise. They yap and snap without end. Dr. Watts said—

> "Let dogs delight to bark and bite,
> For God has made them so."

But I cannot make such an excuse for the two-legged dogs I am writing about, for their own vile tempers, and the devil together, have made them what they are. They find fault with anything and everything. When they dare they howl, and when they cannot do that they lie down and growl inwardly. Beware of these creatures. Make no friends with an angry man: as well make a bed of stinging nettles or wear a viper for a necklace. Perhaps the fellow is just now very fond of you, but beware of him, for he who barks at others to-day without a cause will one day howl at you for nothing. Don't offer him a kennel down your yard unless he will let you chain him up. When you see that a man has a bitter spirit, and gives nobody a good word, quietly walk away and keep out of his track if you can. Loaded guns and quick tempered people are dangerous pieces of furniture; they don't mean any hurt, but they are apt to go off and do mischief before you dream of it. Better go a mile out of your way than get into a fight; better sit down on a dozen tin-tacks with their points up than dispute with an angry neighbour.

Thirdly, *beware of fawning dogs*. They jump up upon you and leave the marks of their dirty paws. How they will lick your hand and fondle you as long as there are bones to be got: like the lover who said to the cook, "Leave you, dear girl? Never, while you have a shilling." Too much sugar in the talk should lead us to suspect that there is very little in the heart. The moment a man praises you to your face, mark him, for he is the very gentleman to rail at you behind your back. If a fellow takes the trouble to flatter he expects to be paid for it, and he calculates that he will get his wages out of the soft brains of those he tickles. When people stoop down it generally is to pick something up, and men don't stoop to flatter you unless they reckon upon getting something out of you. When you see too much politeness you may generally smell a rat if you give a good sniff. Young people need to be on the watch against crafty flatterers. Young women with pretty faces and a little money should especially *beware of puppies*!

Fourthly, *beware of a greedy dog*, or a man who never has enough. Grumbling is catching; one discontented man sets others complaining, and this is a bad state of mind to fall into. Folks who are greedy are not always honest, and if they see a chance they will put their spoon into their neighbour's porridge; why not into yours? See how cleverly they skin a flint; before long you will find them skinning you, and as you are not quite so used to it as the eels are, you had better give Mr. Skinner a wide berth. When a man boasts that he never gives anything away, you may read it as a caution —"beware of the dog." A liberal, kind-hearted friend helps you to keep down your selfishness, but a greedy grasper tempts you to put an extra button on your pocket. Hungry dogs will wolf down any quantity of meat, and then look out for more, and so will greedy men swallow farms and houses, and then smell around for something else. I am sick of the animals: I mean both the dogs and the men. Talking of nothing but gold, and how to make money, and how to save it— why one had better live with the hounds at once, and howl over your share of dead horse. The mischief a miserly wretch may do to a man's heart no tongue can tell; one might as well be bitten by a mad dog, for greediness is as bad a madness as a mortal can be tormented with. Keep out of the company of screw-drivers, tight-fists, hold-fasts, and blood-suckers: "beware of dogs."

Fifthly, *beware of a yelping dog.* Those who talk much tell a great many lies, and if you love truth you had better not love *them.* Those who talk much are likely enough to speak ill of their neighbours, and of yourself among the rest; and therefore, if you do not want to be town-talk, you will be wise to find other friends. Mr. Prate-apace will weary you out one day, and you will be wise to break off his acquaintance before it is made. Do not lodge in Clack Street, or next door to the Gossip's Head. A lion's jaw is nothing compared to a tale-bearer's. If you have a dog which is always barking, and should chance to lose him, don't spend a penny in advertising for him. Few are the blessings which are poured upon dogs which howl all night and wake up honest householders, but even these can be better put up with than those incessant chatterers who never let a man's character rest either day or night.

Sixthly, *beware of a dog that worries the sheep.* Such get into our churches, and cause a world of misery. Some have new doctrines as rotten as they are new; others have new plans, whims, and crotchets, and nothing will go right till these are tried; and there is a third sort, which are out of love with everybody and everything, and only come into the churches to see if they can make a row. Mark these, and keep clear of them. There are plenty of humble Christians who only want leave to be quiet and mind their own business, and these troublers are their plague. To hear the gospel, and to be helped to do good, is all that the most of our members want, but these worries come in with their "ologies" and puzzlements, and hard speeches, and cause sorrow upon sorrow. A good shepherd will soon fetch these dogs a crack of the head; but they will be at their work again if they see half a chance. What pleasure can they find in it? Surely they must have a touch of the wolf in their nature. At any rate, beware of the dog.

Seventhly, *beware of dogs who have returned to their vomit.* An apostate is like a leper. As a rule none are more bitter enemies of the cross than those who once professed to be followers of Jesus. He who can turn away from Christ is not a fit companion for any honest man. There are many abroad nowadays who have thrown off religion as easily as a ploughman puts off his jacket. It will be a terrible day for them when the heavens are on fire above them, and the world is ablaze under their feet. If a man calls himself my friend, and leaves the ways of God, then his way and mine are different; he who is no friend to the good cause is no friend of mine.

Lastly, finally, and to finish up, *beware of a dog that has no master.* If a fellow makes free with the Bible, and the laws of his country, and common decency, it is time to make free to tell him we had rather have his room than his company. A certain set of wonderfully wise men are talking very big things, and putting their smutty fingers upon everything which their fathers thought to be good and holy. Poor fools, they are not half as clever as they think they are. Like hogs in a flower-garden, they are for rooting up everything; and some people are so frightened that they stand as if they were stuck, and hold up their hands in horror at the creatures. When the hogs have been in my master's garden, and I have had the big whip handy, I warrant you I have made a clearance, and I only wish I was a scholar, for I would lay about me among these free-thinking gentry, and make them squeal to a long metre tune. As John Ploughman has other fish to fry, and other tails to butter, he must leave these mischievous creatures, and finish his rough ramshackle sermon.

"Beware of the dog." Beware of all who will do you harm. Good company is to be had, why seek bad? It is said of heaven, "without are dogs." Let us make friends of those who can go inside of heaven, for there we hope to go ourselves. We shall go to our own company when we die; let it be such that we shall be glad to go to it.

LIKE CAT LIKE KIT

OST men are what their mothers made them. The father is away from home all day, and has not half the influence over the children that the mother has. The cow has most to do with the calf. If a ragged colt grows into a good horse, we know who it is that combed him. A mother is therefore a very responsible woman, even though she may be the poorest in the land, for the bad or the good of her boys and girls very much depends upon her. As is the gardener such is the garden, as is the wife such is the family. Samuel's mother made him a little coat every year, but she had done a deal for him before that: Samuel would not have been Samuel if Hannah had not been Hannah. We shall never see a better set of men till the mothers are better. We must have Sarahs and Rebekahs before we shall see Isaacs and Jacobs. Grace does not run in the blood, but we generally find that the Timothys have mothers of a godly sort.

Little children give their mother the headache, but if she lets them have their own way, when they grow up to be great children they will give her the heartache. Foolish fondness spoils many, and letting faults alone spoils more. Gardens that are never weeded will grow very little worth gathering; all watering and no hoeing will make a bad crop. A child may have too much of its mother's love, and in the long run it may turn out that it had too little. Soft-hearted mothers rear soft-headed children; they hurt them for life because they are afraid of hurting them when they are young. Coddle your children, and they will turn out noodles. You may sugar a child till everybody is sick of it. Boys' jackets need a little dusting every now and then, and girls' dresses are all the better for occasional trimming. Children without chastisement are fields without ploughing. The very best colts want breaking in. Not that we like severity; cruel mothers are not mothers, and those who are always flogging and fault-finding ought to be flogged themselves. There is reason in all things, as the madman said when he cut off his nose.

Good mothers are very dear to their children. There's no mother in the world like our own mother. My friend Sanders, from Glasgow, says, "The mither's breath is aye sweet." Every woman is a handsome woman to her own son. That man is not worth hanging who does not love his mother. When good women lead their little ones to the Saviour, the Lord Jesus blesses not only the children, but their mothers as well. Happy are they among women who see their sons and their daughters walking in the truth.

He who thinks it easy to bring up a family never had one of his own. A mother who trains her children aright had need be wiser than Solomon, for his son turned out a fool. Some children are perverse from their infancy; none are born perfect, but some have a double share of imperfections. Do what you will with some children, they don't improve. Wash a dog, comb a dog, still a dog is but a dog: trouble seems thrown away on some children. Such cases are meant to drive us to God, for he can turn blackamoors white, and cleanse out the leopard's spots. It is clear that whatever faults our children have, we are their parents, and we cannot find fault with the stock they came of. Wild geese do not lay tame eggs. That which is born of a hen will be sure to scratch in the dust. The child of a cat will hunt after mice. Every creature follows its kind. If we are black, we cannot blame our offspring if they are dark too. Let us do our best with them, and pray the Mighty Lord to put his hand to the work. Children of prayer will grow up to be children of praise; mothers who have wept before God for their sons, will one day sing a new song over them. Some colts often break the halter, and yet become quiet in harness. God can make those new whom we cannot mend, therefore let mothers never despair of their children as long as they live. Are they away from you across the sea? Remember, the Lord is there as well as here. Prodigals may wander, but they are never out of sight of the Great Father, even though they may be "a great way off."

Let mothers labour to make home the happiest place in the world. If they are always nagging and grumbling they will lose their hold of their children, and the boys will be tempted to spend their evenings away from home. Home is the best place for boys and men, and a good mother is the soul of home. The smile of a mother's face has enticed many into the right path, and the fear of bringing a tear into her eye has called off many a man from evil ways. The boy may have a heart of iron, but his mother can hold him like a magnet. The devil never reckons a man to be lost so long as he has a good mother alive. O woman, great is thy power! See to it that it be used for him who thought of his mother even in the agonies of death.

A HORSE WHICH CARRIES A HALTER
IS SOON CAUGHT

WITH a few oats in a sieve the nag is tempted, and the groom soon catches him if he has his halter on; but the other horse, who has no rope dangling from his head, gives master Bob a sight of his heels, and away he scampers. To my mind, a man who drinks a glass or two, and goes now and then to the tap-room, is a horse with his bridle on, and stands a fair chance of being locked up in Sir John Barleycorn's stables, and made to carry Madame Drink and her habit. There's nothing like coming out fair and square, and standing free as the air. Plenty will saddle you if they can catch you; don't give them the ghost of a chance. A bird has not got away as long as there is even a thread tied to its leg.

> "I've taken the pledge and I will not falter;
> I'm out in the field and I carry no halter;
> I'm a lively nag that likes plenty of room,
> So I'm not going down to the 'Horse and Groom.'"

In other concerns it is much the same: you can't get out of a bad way without leaving it altogether, bag and baggage. Half-way will never pay. One thing or the other: be an out-and-outer, or else keep in altogether. Shut up the shop and quit the trade if it is a bad one: to close the front shutters and serve customers at the back door is a silly attempt to cheat the devil, and it will never answer. Such hide-and-seek behaviour shows that your conscience has just enough light for you to read your own condemnation by it. Mind what you are at, don't dodge like a rat.

I am always afraid of the tail end of a habit. A man who is always in debt will never be cured till he has paid the last sixpence. When a clock says "tick" once, it will say the same again unless it is quite stopped. Harry Higgins says he only owes for one week at the grocer's, and I am as sure as quarter-day that he will be over head and ears in debt before long. I tell him to clean off the old score and have done with it altogether. He says the tradespeople like to have him on their books, but I am quite sure no man in his senses dislikes ready money. I want him to give up the credit system, for if he does not he will need to outrun the constable.

Bad companions are to be left at once. There's no use in shilly-shallying; they must be told that we would sooner have their room than their company, and if they call again we must start them off with a flea in each ear. Somehow I can't get young fellows to come right out from the black lot; they think they can play with fire and not be burned. Scripture says, "Ye fools, when will ye be wise?"

"April the first stands, mark'd by custom's rules,
A day for being, and for making, fools;
But, pray, what custom, or what rule, supplies
A day for making, or for being, wise?"

Nobody wants to keep a little measles or a slight degree of fever. We all want to be quite quit of disease; and so let us try to be rid of every evil habit. What wrong would it be right for us to stick to? Don't let us tempt the devil to tempt us. If we give Satan an inch, he will take a mile. As long as we carry his halter he counts us among his nags. Off with the halter! May the grace of God set us wholly free. Does not Scripture say, "Come out from among them, and be ye separate, and touch not the unclean thing"?

AN OLD FOX IS SHY OF A TRAP

THE old fox knows the trap of old. You don't catch him so easily as you would a cub. He looks sharp at the sharp teeth, and seems to say,

> "Hollo, my old chap,
> I spy out your trap.
> To-day will you fetch me?
> Or wait till you catch me?"

The cat asked the mice to supper, but only the young ones would come to the feast, and they never went home again. "Will you walk into my parlour?" said the spider to the fly, and the silly creature did walk in, and was soon as dead as a door-nail.

What a many traps have been set for some of us. Man-traps and woman-traps; traps to catch us by the eye, by the ear, by the throat, and by the nose; traps for the head and traps for the heart; day traps, and night traps, and traps for any time you like. The baits are of all sorts, alive and dead, male and female, common and particular. We had need be wiser than foxes, or we shall soon hear the snap of the man-trap and feel its teeth.

Beware of beginnings: he who does not take the first wrong step will not take the second. Beware of drops, for the fellows who drink take nothing but a "drop of beer," or "a drop too much." Drop your drop of grog. Beware of him who says "Is it not a little one?" Little sins are the eggs of great sorrows. Beware of lips smeared with honey: see how many flies are caught with sweets. Beware of evil questions which raise needless doubts, and make it hard for a man to trust his Maker. Beware of a bad rich man who is very liberal to you; he will buy you first and sell you afterwards. Beware of a dressy young woman, without a mind or a heart; you may be in a net before you can say Jack Robinson.

> "Pretty fools are no ways rare:
> Wise men will of such beware."

Beware of the stone which you stumbled over the last time you went that way. Beware of the man who never bewares, and beware of the man whom God has marked. Beware of writing your name on the back of a bill, even though your friend tells you ten times over "it is only a matter of form, you know." It is a form which you had better "formally decline," as our school-master says. If you want to be chopped up, put your hand to a bill; but if you want to be secure never stand as security for any living man, woman, child, youth, maiden, cousin, brother, uncle, or mother-in-law. Beware of trusting all your secrets with anybody but your wife. Beware of a man who will lie, a woman who tells tales out of school, a shop-keeper who sends in his bill twice, and a gentleman who will make your fortune if you will find him a few pounds. Beware of a mule's hind foot, a dog's tooth, and a woman's tongue. Last of all, beware of no man more than of yourself, and take heed in this matter many ways, especially as to your talk. Five words cost Zacharias forty weeks' silence. Many are sorry they spoke, but few ever mourn that they held their tongue.

> "Who looks may leap, and save his shins from knocks;
> Who tries may trust, or foulest treachery find;
> He saves his steed who keeps him under locks;
> Who speaks with heed may boldly speak his mind.
>
> But he whose tongue before his wit doth run,
> Oft speaks too soon and grieves when he has done.
> Full oft loose speech hath bound men fast in pain,
> Beware of taking from thy tongue the rein."

A BLACK HEN LAYS A WHITE EGG

THE egg is white enough though the hen is black as a coal. This is a very simple thing, but it has pleased the simple mind of John Ploughman, and made him cheer up when things have gone hard with him. Out of evil comes good, through the great goodness of God. From threatening clouds we get refreshing showers; in dark mines men find bright jewels: and so from our worst troubles come our best blessings. The bitter cold sweetens the ground, and the rough winds fasten the roots of the old oaks. God sends us letters of love in envelopes with black borders. Many a time have I plucked sweet fruit from bramble bushes, and taken lovely roses from among prickly thorns. Trouble is to believing men and women like the sweetbriar in our hedges, and where it grows there is a delicious smell all around if the dew do but fall upon it from above.

Cheer up, mates, all will come right in the end. The darkest night will turn to a fair morning in due time. Only let us trust in God, and keep our heads above the waves of fear. When our hearts are right with God everything is right. Let us look for the silver which lines every cloud, and when we do not see it let us believe that it is there. We are all at school, and our great Teacher writes many a bright lesson on the blackboard of affliction. Scant fare teaches us to live on heavenly bread, sickness bids us send off for the good

Physician, loss of friends makes Jesus more precious, and even the sinking of our spirits brings us to live more entirely upon God. All things are working together for the good of those who love God, and even death itself will bring them their highest gain. Thus the black hen lays a white egg.

> "Since all that I meet shall work for my good,
>   The bitter is sweet, the medicine is food;
>   Though painful at present 'twill cease before long,
>   And then, oh how pleasant the conqueror's song!"

HE LOOKS ONE WAY AND PULLS THE OTHER

HE faces the shore, but he is pulling for the ship: this is the way of those who row in boats and also of a great many who never trust themselves on the water. The boatman is all right, but the hypocrite is all wrong, whatever rites he may practise. I cannot endure Mr. Facing-both-ways, yet he has swarms of cousins.

It is ill to be a saint without and a devil within, to be a servant of Christ before the world in order to serve the ends of self and the devil, while inwardly the heart hates all good things. There are good and bad of all classes, and hypocrites can be found among plough-men as well as among parsons. It used to be so in the olden times, for I remember an old verse which draws out just such a character: the man says,—

> "I'll have a religion all of my own,
> Whether Papist or Protestant shall not be known;
> And if it proves troublesome I will have none."

In our Lord's day many followed him, but it was only for the loaves and fishes: they do say that some in our parish don't go quite so straight as the Jews did, for they go to the church for the loaves, and then go over to the Baptist chapel for the fishes. I don't want to judge, but I certainly do know some who, if they do

" He looks one way and pulls another "

not care much for faith, are always following after charity.

Better die than sell your soul to the highest bidder. Better be shut up in the workhouse than fatten upon hypocrisy. Whatever else we barter, let us never try to turn a penny by religion, for hypocrisy is the meanest vice a man can come to.

It is a base thing to call yourself Christ's horse and yet carry the devil's saddle. The worst kind of wolf is that which wears a sheep's skin. Jezebel was never so ugly as when she had finished painting her face. Above all things, then, brother labourers, let us be straight as an arrow, and true as a die, and never let us be time-servers, or turn-coats. Never let us carry two faces under one hat, nor blow hot and cold with the same breath.

STICK TO IT AND DO IT

SET a stout heart to a stiff hill, and the waggon will get to the top of it. There's nothing so hard but a harder thing will get through it; a strong job can be managed by a strong resolution. Have at it and have it. Stick to it and succeed. Till a thing is done men wonder that you think it can be done, and when you have done it they wonder it was never done before.

Sometimes we see a waggon drawn by two horses; but I would have every man who wants to make his way in life pull as if all depended on himself. Very little is done right when it is left to other people. The more hands to do work the less there is done. One man will carry two pails of water for himself; two men will only carry one pail between them, and three will come home with never a drop at all. A child with several mothers will die before it runs alone. Know your business and give your mind to it, and you will find a buttered loaf where a sluggard loses his last crust.

In these times it's no use being a farmer if you don't mean work. The days are gone by for gentlemen to make a fortune off a farm by going out shooting half their time. If foreign wheats keep on coming in, farmers will soon learn that—

> "He who by the plough would thrive,
> Himself must either hold or drive."

Going to Australia is of no use to a man if he carries a set of lazy bones with him. There's a living to be got in old England at almost any trade if a fellow will give his mind to it. A man who works hard and has his health and strength is a great deal happier than my lord Tom Noddy, who does nothing and is always ailing. Do you know the old song of "The Nobleman's generous kindness"? You should hear our Will sing it. I recollect some of the verses. The first one gives a picture of the hard-working labourer with a large family—

> "Thus careful and constant, each morning he went,
>   Unto his day labour with joy and content;
>   So jocular and jolly he'd whistle and sing,
>   As blithe and as brisk as the birds in the spring."

The other lines are the ploughman's own story of how he spent his life, and I wish that all countrymen could say the same.

> "I reap and I mow, I harrow and I sow,
>   Sometimes a hedging and ditching I go;
>   No work comes amiss, for I thrash and I plough,
>   Thus my bread I do earn by the sweat of my brow.

> "My wife she is willing to pull in a yoke,
>   We live like two lambs, nor each other provoke;
>   We both of us strive, like the labouring ant,
>   And do our endeavours to keep us from want.

> "And when I come home from my labour at night,
>   To my wife and my children in whom I delight,
>   I see them come round me with prattling noise.
>   Now these are the riches a poor man enjoys.

> "Though I am as weary as weary may be,
>   The youngest I commonly dance on my knee;
>   I find in content a continual feast,
>   And never repine at my lot in the least."

So, you see, the poor labourer may work hard and be happy all the same; and surely those who are in higher stations may do the like if they like.

He is a sorry dog who wants game and will not hunt for it; let us never lie down in idle despair, but follow on till we succeed.

Rome was not built in a day, nor much else, unless it be a dog-kennel. Things which cost no pains are slender gains. Where there has been little sweat there will be little sweet. Jonah's gourd came up in a night, but then it perished in a night. Light come, light go: that which flies in at one window will be likely to fly out at another. It's a very lean hare that hounds catch without running for it, and a sheep that is no trouble to shear has very little wool. For this reason a man who cannot push on against wind and weather stands a poor chance in this world.

Perseverance is the main thing in life. To hold on, and hold out to the end, is the chief matter. If the race could be won by a spurt, thousands would wear the blue ribbon; but they are short-winded and pull up after the first gallop. They begin with flying, and end in crawling backwards. When it comes to collar work, many horses turn to jibbing. If the apples do not fall at the first shake of the tree your hasty folks are too lazy to fetch a ladder, and in too much of a hurry to wait till the fruit is ripe enough to fall of itself. The hasty man is as hot as fire at the outset, and as cold as ice at the end. He is like the Irishman's saucepan, which had many good points about it, but it had no bottom. He who cannot bear the burden and heat of the day is not worth his salt, much less his potatoes.

Before you begin a thing, make sure it is the right thing to do: ask Mr. Conscience about it. Do not try to do what is impossible: ask Common Sense. It is of no use to blow against a hurricane, or to fish for whales in a washing tub. Better give up a foolish plan than go on and burn your fingers with it: better bend your neck than knock your forehead. But when you have once made up your mind to go a certain road, don't let every molehill turn you out of the path. One stroke fells not an oak. Chop away, axe, you'll down with the tree at last! A bit of iron does not soften the moment you put it into the fire. Blow, smith! Put on more coals! Get it red-hot and hit hard with the hammer, and you will make a ploughshare yet. Steady does it. Hold on and you have it. Brag is a fine fellow at crying "Tally-ho!" but Perseverance brings home the brush.

We ought not to be put out of heart by difficulties: they are sent on purpose to try the stuff we are made of; and depend upon it they do us a world of good. There's a sound reason why there are bones in our meat and stones in our land. A world where everything was easy would be a nursery for babies, but not at all a fit place for men. Celery is not sweet till it has felt a frost, and men don't come to their perfection till disappointment has dropped a half-hundred weight or two on their toes. Who would know good horses if there were no heavy loads? If the clay was not stiff, my old Dapper and Violet would be thought no more of than Tomkins' donkey. Besides, to work hard for success makes us fit to bear it: we enjoy the bacon all the more because we have got an appetite by earning it. When prosperity pounces on a man like an eagle, it often throws him

down. If we overtake the cart, it is a fine thing to get
up and ride; but when it comes behind us at a tearing
rate, it is very apt to knock us down and run over us,
and when we are lifted into it we find our leg is broken,
or our arm out of joint, and we cannot enjoy the ride.
Work is always healthier for us than idleness; it is
always better to wear out shoes than sheets. I sometimes think, when I put on my considering cap, that
success in life is something like getting married: there's
a very great deal of pleasure in the courting, and it is
not a bad thing when it is a moderate time on the road.
Therefore, young man, learn to wait, and work on.
Don't throw away your rod, the fish will bite some
time or other. The cat watches long at the hole, but
catches the mouse at last. The spider mends her broken
web, and the flies are taken before long. Stick to your
calling, plod on, and be content; for, make sure, if
you can *undergo* you shall *overcome*.

> If bad be your prospects, don't sit still and cry,
> But jump up, and say to yourself, "I WILL TRY."

Miracles will never cease! My neighbour, Simon
Gripper, was taken generous about three months ago.
The story is well worth telling. He saw a poor blind
man, led by a little girl, playing on a fiddle. His heart
was touched, for a wonder. He said to me, "Ploughman,
lend me a penny, there's a good fellow." I fumbled in
my pocket, and found two halfpence, and handed them
to him. More fool I, for he will never pay me again.
He gave the blind fiddler one of those halfpence, and
kept the other, and I have not seen either Gripper or
my penny since, nor shall I get the money back till

the gate-post outside my garden grows Ribstone pippins. There's generosity for you! The old saying which is put at the top of this bit of my talk brought him into my mind, for he *sticks to it* most certainly: he lives as badly as a church mouse, and works as hard as if he was paid by the piece, and had twenty children to keep; but I would no more hold him up for an example than I would show a toad as a specimen of a pretty bird. While I talk to you young people about getting on, I don't want you to think that hoarding up money is real success; nor do I wish you to rise an inch above an honest ploughman's lot, if it cannot be done without being mean or wicked. The workhouse, prison as it is, is a world better than a mansion built by roguery and greed. If you cannot get on honestly, be satisfied not to get on. The blessing of God is riches enough for a wise man, and all the world is not enough for a fool. Old Gripper's notion of how to prosper has, I dare say, a good deal of truth in it, and the more's the pity. The Lord deliver us from such a prospering, I say. That old sinner has often hummed these lines into my ears when we have got into an argument, and very pretty lines they are *not*, certainly:—

> "To win the prize in the world's great race
> A man should have a brazen face;
> An iron arm to give a stroke,
> And a heart as sturdy as an oak;
> Eyes like a cat, good in the dark,
> And teeth as piercing as a shark;
> Ears to hear the gentlest sound,
> Like moles that burrow in the ground;
> A mouth as close as patent locks,
> And stomach stronger than an ox;

His tongue should be a razor-blade,
His conscience india-rubber made;
His blood as cold as polar ice,
His hand as grasping as a vice.
His shoulders should be adequate
To bear a couple thousand weight;
His legs, like pillars, firm and strong,
To move the great machine along;
With supple knees to cringe and crawl,
And cloven feet placed under all."

It amounts to this: be a devil in order to be happy. Sell yourself outright to the old dragon, and he will give you the world and the glory thereof. But remember the question of the Old Book, "What shall it profit a man, if he gain the whole world, and lose his own soul?" There is another road to success besides this crooked, dirty, cut-throat lane. It is the King's highway, of which the same Book says: "Seek ye first the kingdom of God, and his righteousness; and all these things shall be added unto you." John Ploughman prays that all his readers may choose this way, and keep to it; yet even in that way we must use diligence, "for the kingdom of heaven suffereth violence, and the violent take it by force."

DON'T PUT THE CART BEFORE THE HORSE

NOBODY will ever take that fellow to be a
Solomon. He has no more sense than a sucking
turkey; his wit will never kill him, but he may
die for want of it. One would think that he does not
know which side of himself goes first, or which end
should be uppermost, for he is putting the cart before
the horse. However, he is not the only fool in the world,
for nowadays you can't shake your coat out of a window
without dusting an idiot. You have to ask yourself
what will be the next new piece of foolery.

Amusing blunders will happen. Down at our chapel
we only have evening meetings on moonlight nights,
for some of our friends would never find their way home
down our Surrey lanes of a dark night. It is a long lane
that has no turning, but ours have plenty of turnings,
and are quite as long as one likes them when it is pitch
dark, for the trees meet over your head and won't let a
star peep through. What did our old clerk do the other
Sunday but give notice that there would be no moon
next Wednesday night in consequence of there being
no service. He put the cart before the horse that time.
So it was with the young parson, of very fine ideas, who
tried to make us poor clod-hoppers see the wisdom
of Providence in making the great rivers run near the
large towns, while our village had a small brook to suit
the size of it. We had a quiet laugh at the good man as we

walked home through the corn, and we wondered why it never occurred to him that the Thames was in its bed long before London was up, and our tiny stream ran through its winding ways long before a cottager dipped his pail into it.

Dick Widgeon had a married daughter who brought her husband as pretty a baby as one might wish to see. When it was born, a neighbour asked the old man whether it was a boy or a girl. "Dear, dear," said Dick, "here's a kettle of fish! I'm either a grandfather or a grandmother, and I'm sure I don't know which." Dick says his mother was an Irishman, but I do not believe it.

All this is fun, but some of this blundering leads to mischief. Lazy fellows ruin their trade, and then say that bad trade ruined them.

Some fellows talk at random, as if they lived in a world turned upside down, for they always put things the wrong side up. A serving-man lost his situation through his drunken ways; and, as he could get no character, he charged his old master with being his ruin.

> "Robert complained the other day
> His master took his character away;
> 'I take your character,' said he, 'no fear,
> Not for a thousand pounds a year.' "

The man was his own downfall, and now he blames those who speak the truth about him. "He mistakes the effect for the cause," as our old schoolmaster says, and blames the bucket for the faults of the well.

The other day a fellow said to me, "Don't you think

Jones is a lucky chap?" "No," said I, "I think he is a hard-working man, and gets on because he deserves it." "Ah," was the man's answer, "don't tell me; he has got a good trade, and a capital shop, and a fair capital, and I don't wonder that he makes money." Bless the man's heart; Jones began with nothing, in a little, poking shop, and all he has was scraped together by hard labour and careful saving. The shop would never have kept him if he had not kept the shop, and he would have had no trade if he had not been a good tradesman; but there, it's no use talking, some people will never allow that thrift and temperance lead to thriving and comfort, for this would condemn themselves. So to quiet their consciences they put the cart before the horse.

A very bad case of putting the cart before the horse is when a drinking old man talks as if he had been kept out of the grave by his beer, though that is the thing which carries people to their last home. He happens to have a strong constitution, and so he can stand the effects of drink better than most, and then folks say it was the drink which gave him the constitution. When an old soldier comes alive out of battle, do we think that the shot and shell saved his life? When we meet with a man who is so strong that he can be a great drinker and still seem little the worse, we must not say that he owes his strength to his beer, or we shall be putting the plough before the oxen.

When a man thinks that he is to make himself good before he comes to Jesus to be saved, he is planting the fruit instead of the root; and putting the chimney pots where the foundation should be. We do not save ourselves and then trust the Saviour; but when the Saviour has worked salvation in us, then we work it out with fear and trembling. Be sure, good reader, that you put faith first, and works afterwards; for if not, you will put the cart before the horse.

A LEAKING TAP IS A GREAT WASTER

A LEAKING tap is a great waster. Drop by drop, by day and by night, the liquor runs away, and the housewife wonders how so much can have gone. This is the fashion in which many labouring men are kept poor: they don't take care of the pence, and so they have no pounds to put in the bank. You cannot fill the rain-water butt if you do not catch the drops. A sixpence here, and a shilling there, and his purse is empty before a man dares to look in it. What with waste in the kitchen, waste at table, and waste at the public-house, fools and their money soon part to meet no more. If the wife wastes too, there are two holes in the barrel. Sometimes the woman dresses in tawdry finery and gets in debt to the tally-man; and it is still worse if she takes to the bottle. When the goose drinks as deep as the gander, pots are soon empty, and the cupboard is bare. Then they talk about saving, like the man who locked the stable door after his horse was stolen. They will not save at the brim, but promise themselves and the pigs that they will do wonders when they get near the bottom. It is well to follow the good old rule:—

> "Spend so as ye may
> Spend for many a day."

He who eats all the loaf at breakfast may whistle for his dinner, and get a dish of empties. If we do not save while we have it, we certainly shall not save after all is gone. There is no grace in waste. Economy is a duty; extravagance is a sin. The old Book saith, "He that hasteth to be rich shall not be innocent," and, depend upon it, he that hasteth to be poor is in much the same box. Stretch your legs according to the length of your blanket, and never spend all that you have:

> "Put a little by;
> Things may go awry."

It will help to keep you from anxious care—which is sinful, if you take honest care—which is commendable. Lay up when young, and you shall find when old; but do not this greedily, or selfishly, or God may send a curse on your store. Money is not a comfort by itself, for they said in the olden time—

> "They who have money are troubled about it,
> And they who have none are troubled without it."

But though the dollar is not almighty, it ought to be used *for* the Almighty, and not wasted in wicked extravagance. Even a dog will hide up a bone which he does not want, and it is said of wolves that they gnaw not the bones till the morrow; but many of our working men are without thrift or forethought, and, like children, they will eat all the cake at once if they can. When a frost comes they are poor frozen-out gardeners, and ask for charity, when they ought to have laid up for a snowy day. I wonder they are not ashamed of themselves. Those are three capital lines:—

> "Earn all you can,
> Save all you can,
> Give all you can."

But our neighbour Scroggs acts on quite a different rule-of-three, and tries three other cans:

> "Eat all you can,
> Drink all you can,
> Spend all you can."

He can do more of all these than is canny; it would be a good thing if he and the beer-can were a good deal further apart.

I don't want any person to become a screw, or a hoarder, or a lover of money, but I do wish our working men would make better use of what they get. It is little enough, I know; but some make it less by squandering it. Solomon commends the good woman who "considereth a field and buyeth it: with the fruit of her hands she planteth a vineyard;" he also tells the sluggard to go to the ant, and see how she stores for the winter. I am told that ants of this sort do not live in England, and I am afraid they don't; but my master says he has seen them in France, and I think it would be a good idea to bring over the breed. My old friend Tusser says,—

> "Ill husbandry drinketh
> Himself out of door;
> Good husbandry thinketh
> Of friend and of poor."

The more of such good husbandry the merrier for old England. You cannot burn your faggots in autumn and then stack them for the winter; if you want the calf to become a cow, you must not be in a hurry to eat neats' feet. Money once spent is like shot fired from a gun, you can never call it back. No matter how sorry you may be, the goldfinches are out of the cage, and they will not fly back for all your crying. If a fellow gets into debt it is worse still, for that is a ditch in which many find mud, but none catch fish. When all his sugar is gone, a man's friends are not often very sweet upon him. People who have nothing are very apt to be thought worth nothing: mind, *I* don't say so, but a good many do. Wrinkled purses make wrinkled faces. It has been said that they laugh most who have least to lose, and it may be so; but I am afraid that some of them laugh on the wrong side of their faces. Foolish spending buys a pennyworth of merry-making, but it costs many a pound of sorrow. The profligate sells his cow to buy a canary, and boils down a bullock to get half-a-pint of bad soup, and that he throws away as soon as he has tasted it. I should not care to spend all my living to buy a mouldy repentance, yet this is what many a prodigal has done, and many more will do.

My friend, keep money in thy purse: "It is one of Solomon's proverbs," said one; another answered that it was not there. "Then," said Kit Lancaster, "it might have been, and if Solomon had ever known the miss of a shilling he would have said it seven times over." I think that he does say as much as this in substance, if not in so many words, especially when he talks about the ant; but be that how it may, be sure of this, that a pound in the pocket is as good as a friend at court, and rather better; and if ever you live to want what you once wasted, it will fill you with woe enough to last you to your grave. He who put a pound of butter on a grid-iron, not only lost his butter, but made such a blaze as he won't soon forget: foolish lavishness leads to dreadful wickedness, so John Ploughman begs all his mates to fight shy of it, and post off to the Post Office Savings' Bank.

> "For age and want save while you may;
> No morning's sun lasts all the day."

Money is not the chief thing, it is as far below the grace of God and faith in Christ as a ploughed field is below the stars; but still, godliness hath the promise of the life that now is as well as of that which is to come, and he who is wise enough to seek first the kingdom of God and his righteousness, should also be wise enough to use aright the other things which God is pleased to add unto him.

Somewhere or other I met with a set of mottoes about gold, which I copied out, and here they are: I don't know who first pricked them down, but like a great many of the things which are stuck together in my books, I found them here and there, and they are none of mine: at least, I cannot claim the freehold, but have them on copyhold, which is a fair tenure. If the owners of these odds and ends will call for them at the house where this book is published they may have them on paying a shilling for the paper they are done up in.

MOTTOES ABOUT GOLD.

A vain man's motto is ...... "Win gold and wear it."
A generous man's motto is .. "Win gold and share it."
A miserly man's motto is .... "Win gold and spare it."
A profligate man's motto is .. "Win gold and spend it."
A banker's motto is .... "Win gold and lend it."
A gambler's motto is ...... "Win gold or lose it."
A wise man's motto is ...... "Win gold and use it."

FOOLS SET STOOLS FOR WISE MEN TO STUMBLE OVER

THIS is what they call "a lark." Fools set stools for wise men to stumble over. To ask questions is as easy as kissing your hand; to answer them is hard as fattening a grey-hound. Any fool can throw a stone into a deep well, and the cleverest man in the parish may never be able to get it up again. Folly grows in all countries, and fools are all the world over, as he said who shod the goose. Silly people are pleased with their own nonsense, and think it rare fun to quiz their betters. To catch a wise man tripping is as good as bowling a fellow out at a cricket-match.

> "Folly is wise in her own eyes,
> Therefore she tries Wit to surprise."

There are difficulties in everything except in eating pancakes, and nobody ought to be expected to untie all the knots in a net, or to make that straight which God has made crooked. He is the greatest fool of all who pretends to explain everything, and says he will not believe what he cannot understand. There are bones in the meat, but am I to go hungry till I can eat them? Must I never enjoy a cherry till I find one without a stone? John Ploughman is not of that mind. He is under no call to doubt, for he is not a doctor: when people try to puzzle him he tells them that those who made the lock had better make the key, and those who

" Fools set stools "

put the cow in the pound had better get her out. Then they get cross, and John only says—You need not be crusty, for you are none too much baked.

After all, what do we know if all our knowing was put together? It would all go in a thimble, and the girl's finger, too. A very small book would hold most men's learning, and every line would have a mistake in it. Why, then, should we spend our lives in perplexity, tumbling about like pigs in a sack, and wondering how we shall ever get out again? John knows enough to know that he does not know enough to explain all that he knows, and so he leaves the stools to the schools and the other —ools.

A MAN IN A PASSION RIDES A HORSE THAT RUNS AWAY WITH HIM

WHEN passion has run away with a man, who knows where it will carry him? Once let a rider lose power over his horse, and he may go over hedge and ditch, and end with a tumble into the stone-quarry and a broken neck. No one can tell in cold blood what he may do when he gets angry; therefore it is best to run no risks. Those who feel their temper rising will be wise if they rise themselves and walk off to the pump. Let them fill their mouths with cold water, hold it there ten minutes at the least, and then go indoors, and keep there till they feel cool as a cucumber. If you carry loose gunpowder in your pocket, you had better not go where sparks are flying; and if you are bothered with an irritable nature, you should move off when folks begin teasing you. Better keep out of a quarrel than fight your way through it.

Nothing is improved by anger unless it be the arch of a cat's back. A man with his back up is spoiling his figure. People look none the handsomer for being red in the face. It takes a great deal out of a man to get into a towering rage; it is almost as unhealthy as having a fit, and time has been when men have actually choked themselves with passion, and died on the spot. Whatever wrong I suffer, it cannot do me half so much hurt as being angry about it; for passion shortens life and poisons peace.

When once we give way to temper, temper will claim a right of way, and come in easier every time. He that will be in a pet for any little thing will soon be out at elbows about nothing at all. A thunderstorm curdles the milk, and so does a passion sour the heart and spoil the character.

He who is in a tantrum shuts his eyes and opens his mouth, and very soon says what he will be sorry for. Better bite your lips now than smart for life. It is easier to keep a bull out of a china shop than it is to get him out again; and, besides, there's no end of a bill to pay for damages.

A man burning with anger carries a murderer inside his waistcoat; the sooner he can cool down the better for himself and all around him. He will have to give an account for his feelings as well as for his words and actions, and that account will cost him many tears. It is a cruel thing to tease quick-tempered people, for, though it may be sport to you, it is death to them; at least, it is death to their peace, and may be something worse. We know who said, "Woe to that man by whom the offence cometh."

Shun a furious man as you would a mad dog, but do it kindly, or you may make him worse than he would be. Don't put a man out when you know he is out with himself. When his monkey is up be very careful, for he means mischief. A surly soul is sure to quarrel; he says the cat will break his heart, and the coal scuttle will be the death of him.

> "A man in a rage
> Needs a great iron cage.
> He'll tear and he'll dash
> Till he comes to a smash;
> So let's out of his way
> As quick as we may."

As we quietly move off let us pray for the angry person; for a man in a thorough passion is as sad a sight as to see a neighbour's house on fire and no water handy to put out the flames.

Let us wish the fellow on the runaway horse a soft ditch to tumble in, and sense enough never to get on the creature's back again.

WHERE THE PLOUGH SHALL FAIL TO GO, THERE THE WEEDS WILL SURELY GROW

IN my young days farmers used to leave broad headlands; and, as there were plenty of good-for-nothing hedges and ditches, they raised a prime crop of weeds, and these used to sow the farm, and give a heap of trouble. Then Farmer Numskull "never could make out nohow where all they there weeds could 'a come from." In those good old times, as stupids call them, old Tusser said:

> "Slack never thy weeding for dear or for cheap,
> The corn shall reward it when harvest ye reap."

He liked to see weeding done just after rain: no bad judge either. He said,

> "Then after a shower, to weeding a snatch,
> 'Tis more easy then the root to despatch."

Weeding is wanted now, for ill weeds grow apace, and the hoe must always go; but still lands are a fine sight cleaner than they used to be, for now farmers go a deal closer to work, and grub up the hedges, and make large fields, to save every bit of land. Quite right, too. The less there is wasted the more there is for us all.

> To clothe the fields with plenty and all our barns endow,
> We'll turn up every corner and drive the useful plough.
> No weed shall haunt the furrow, before us all shall bow,
> We'll gaily yield our labour to guide the useful plough.

It would be well to do the same thing in other concerns. Depend upon it, weeds will come wherever you give them half a chance. When children have no school to go to they will pretty soon be up to mischief; and if they are not taught the gospel, the old enemy will soon teach them to thieve, and lie, and swear. You can tell with your eyes shut where there's a school and where there's none: only use your ears and hear the young ones talk.

So far goes the plough, and where that leaves off the docks and the thistles begin, as sure as dirt comes where there's no washing, and mice where there are no cats. They tell me that in London and other big towns vice and crime are sure to spread where there are no ragged schools and Sunday schools; and I don't wonder. I hope the day will never come when good people will give up teaching the boys and girls. Keep that plough going, say I, till you have cut up all the charlock. Don't leave a rod of ground for the devil to sow his tares in. In my young time few people in our parish could either read or write, and what were they to do but gossip, and drink and fight, and play old gooseberry? Now that teaching is to be had, people will all be scholars, and, as they can buy a Testament for a penny, I hope they will search the Scriptures, and may God bless the word to the cleansing of their souls. When the schoolmaster gets to his work in downright earnest, I hope and trust there will be a wonderful clearance of the weeds.

The best plough in all the world is the preaching of the gospel. Leave a village without Christ crucified, and it soon becomes a great tangle of thorn, and briar, and brake, and bramble; but when sound and sensible preaching comes, it tears all up like a steam plough, and the change is something to sing about. "The desert shall rejoice and blossom as the rose."

Inside a man's heart there is need of a thorough ploughing by God's grace, for if any part of our nature is left to itself, the weeds of sin will smother the soul. Every day we have need to be looked after, for follies grow in no time, and come to a great head before you can count twenty. God speed the plough.

ALL IS LOST THAT IS POURED INTO A CRACKED DISH

COOK is wasting her precious liquor, for it runs out almost as fast as it runs in. The sooner she stops that game the better. This makes me think of a good deal of preaching, it is labour in vain, because it does not stay in the minds of the hearers, but goes in at one ear and out at the other. When men go to market they are all alive to do a trade, but in a place of worship they are not more than half awake, and do not seem to care whether they profit or not by what they hear. I once heard a preacher say, "Half of you are asleep, half are inattentive, and the rest——." He never finished that sentence, for the people began to smile, and here and there one burst out laughing. Certainly, many only go to meeting to stare about.

> "Attend your church, the parson cries,
>   To church each fair one goes;
> The old ones go to close their eyes,
>   The young to eye their clothes."

You might as well preach to the stone images in the old church as to people who are asleep. Some old fellows come into our meeting, pitch into their corner, and settle themselves down for a quiet snooze as knowingly as if the pew was a sleeping-car on the railway. Still, all the sleeping at service is not the fault of the poor people, for some parsons put a lot of sleeping stuff into their sermons. Will Shepherd says they *mesmerize* the people. (I think that is the right word, but I'm not sure.) I saw a verse in a real live book by Mr. Cheales, the vicar of Brockham, a place which is handy to my home. I'll give it you:

> "The ladies praise our curate's eyes.
> I never see their light divine,
> For when he prays he closes them,
> And when he preaches closes mine."

Well, if curates are heavy in style, the people will soon be heavy in sleep. Even when hearers are awake many of them are forgetful. It is like pouring a jug of ale between the bars of a gridiron, to try and teach them good doctrine. Water on a duck's back does have some effect, but sermons by the hundred are as much lost upon many men's hearts as if they had been spoken to a kennel of hounds. Preaching to some fellows is like whipping the water or lashing the air. As well talk to a turnip, or whistle to a dead donkey, as preach to these dull ears. A year's sermons will not produce an hour's repentance till the grace of God comes in.

We have a good many hangers-on who think that their duty to God consists in hearing sermons, and that the best fruit of their hearing is to talk of what they have heard. How they do lay the law down when they get argifying about doctrines! Their religion all runs to ear and tongue: neither their heart nor their hand is a scrap the better. This is poor work, and will never pay the piper. The sermon which only gets as far as the ear is like a dinner eaten in a dream. It is ill to lie soaking in the gospel like a bit of coal in a milk-pan, never the whiter for it all.

What can be the good of being hearers only? It disappoints the poor preacher, and it brings no blessing to the man himself. Looking at a plum won't sweeten your mouth, staring at a coat won't cover your back, and lying on the bank won't catch the fish in the river. The cracked dish is never the better for all that is poured into it: it is like our forgetful heart, it wants to be taken away, and a new one put instead of it.

GRASP ALL AND LOSE ALL

WHILE so many poor neighbours are around us it is a sin to hoard. If we do we shall be losers, for rats eat corn, rust cankers metal, and the curse of God spoils riches. A tight fist is apt to get the rheumatism, an open hand bears the palm. It is good to give a part to sweeten the rest. A great stack of hay is apt to heat and take fire; cut a piece out and let the air in, and the rest will be safe. What say you, Mr. Reader, to cut a few pounds out of your heap, and send them to help feed the orphans?

SCATTER AND INCREASE

PEOPLE will not believe it, and yet it is true as the gospel, that giving leads to thriving. John Bunyan said,

> "There was a man, and some did count him mad,
> The more he gave away, the more he had."

He had an old saying to back him, one which is as old as the hills, and as good as gold—

> "Give and spend
> And God will send."

If a man cannot pay his debts he must not think of giving, for he has nothing of his own, and it is thieving to give away other people's property. Be just before you are generous. Don't give to Peter what is due to Paul. They used to say that "Give" is dead, and "Restore" is buried, but I do not believe it any more than I do another saying, "There are only two good men, one is dead, and the other is not born." No, no: there are many free hearts yet about, and John Ploughman knows a goodish few of them—people who don't cry, "Go next door," but who say, "Here's a little help, and we wish we could make it ten times as much." God has often a great share in a small house, and many a little man has a large heart.

Now, you will find that liberal people are happy

people, and get more enjoyment out of what they have than folks of a churlish mind. Misers never rest till they are put to bed with a shovel: they often get so wretched that they would hang themselves only they grudge the expense of a rope. Generous souls are made happy by the happiness of others: the money they give to the poor buys them more pleasure than any other that they lay out.

I have seen men of means give coppers, and they have been coppery in everything. They carried on a tin-pot business, lived like beggars, and died like dogs. I have seen others give to the poor and to the cause of God by shovelfuls and they have had it back by barrow-loads. They made good use of their stewardship, and the great Lord has trusted them with more, while the bells in their hearts have rung out merry peals when they have thought of widows who blessed them, and orphan children who smiled into their faces. Ah me, that there should be creatures in the shape of men whose souls are of no use except as salt to keep their bodies from rotting! Please let us forget them, for it makes me feel right down sick to think of their nasty ways. Let us see what we can do to scatter joy all around us, just as the sun throws his light on hill and dale. He that gives God his heart will not deny him his money. He will take a pleasure in giving, but he will not wish to be seen, nor will he expect to have a pound of honour for sixpence. He will look out for worthy objects; for giving to lazy, drunken spendthrifts is wasteful and wicked; you might as well sugar a brickbat and think to turn it into a pudding. A wise man will go to work in a sensible way, and will so give his money to the poor that he will be lending it to the Lord. No security can be better and no interest can be surer. The Bank is open at all hours. It is the best Savings' Bank in the world.

EVERY BIRD LIKES ITS OWN NEST

IT pleases me to see how fond the birds are of their little homes. No doubt each one thinks his own nest is the very best; and so it is for him, just as my home is the best palace for me, even for me King John, the king of the Cottage of Content. I will ask no more if providence only continues to give me—

> "A little field well tilled,
> A little house well filled,
> And a little wife well willed."

An Englishman's house is his castle, and the true Briton is always fond of the old roof-tree. Green grows the house-leek on the thatch, and sweet is the honey-suckle at the porch, and dear are the gilly-flowers in the front garden; but best of all is the good wife within, who keeps all as neat as a new pin. Frenchmen may live in their coffee-houses, but an Englishman's best life is seen at home.

> "My own house, though small,
> Is the best house of all."

When boys get tired of eating tarts, and maids have done with winning hearts, and lawyers cease to take their fees, and leaves leave off to grow on trees, then will John Ploughman cease to love his own dear home. John likes to hear some sweet voice sing—

> "'Mid pleasures and palaces though we may roam,
>   Be it ever so humble, there's no place like home;
>   A charm from the sky seems to hallow us there,
>   Which, wherever we rove, is not met with elsewhere.
>
>   Home! Home! sweet, sweet home!
>   There's no place like home!"

People who take no pleasure in their own homes are queer folks, and no better than they should be. Every dog is a lion at his own door, and a man should make most of those who make most of him. Women should be house-keepers and keep in the house. That man is to be pitied who has married one of the Miss Gadabouts. Mrs. Cackle and her friend Mrs. Dressemout are enough to drive their husbands into the county jail for shelter: there can be no peace where such a piece of goods as either of them is to be found. Old Tusser said—

> "Ill huswifery pricketh
>   Herself up with pride:
>   Good huswifery tricketh
>   Her house as a bride.
>
> "Ill huswifery moveth
>   With gossip to spend:
>   Good huswifery loveth
>   Her household to tend."

The woman whose husband wastes his evenings with low fellows at the beer-shop is as badly off as a slave; and when the Act of Parliament shuts up most of these ruin-houses, it will be an Act of Emancipation for her. Good husbands cannot have too much of their homes, and if their wives make their homes comfortable they will soon grow proud of them. When good fathers get among their children they are as merry as mice in malt. Our Joe Scroggs says he's tired of his house, and the house certainly looks tired of him, for it is all out of windows, and would get out of doors if it knew how. He will never be weary in well doing, for he never began. What a different fellow he would be if he could believe that the best side of the world is a man's own fireside. I know it is so, and so do many more.

> "Seek home for rest,
> For home is best."

What can it be that so deludes lots of people who ought to know better? They have sweet wives, and nice families, and comfortable houses, and they are several cuts above us poor country bumpkins, and yet they must be out of an evening. What is it for? Surely it can't be the company; for the society of the woman you love, who is the mother of your children, is worth all the companies that ever met together. I fear they are away soaking their clay, and washing all their wits away. If so, it is a great shame, and those who are guilty of it ought to be trounced. O that drink! that drink!

Dear, dear, what stuff people will pour into their insides! Even if I had to be poisoned I should like to know what I was swallowing. A cup of tea at home does people a sight more good than all the mixtures you get abroad. There's nothing like the best home-brewed, and there's no better mash-tub for making it in than the old-fashioned earthenware teapot. Our little children sing, "Please, father, come home," and John Ploughman joins with thousands of little children in that simple prayer which every man who is a man should be glad to answer. I like to see husband and wife longing to see each other.

> "An ear that waits to catch,
>   A hand upon the latch;
> A step that hastens its sweet rest to win;
>   A world of care without,
>   A world of strife shut out,
>   A world of love shut in."

Fellow workmen, try to let it be so with you and your wives. Come home, and bring your wages with you, and make yourselves happy by making everyone happy around you.

My printer jogs my elbow, and says, "That will do: I can't get any more in." Then, Mr. Passmore, I must pass over many things, but I cannot leave off without praising God for his goodness to me and mine, and all my brother ploughmen, for it is of his great mercy that he lets us live in this dear old country and loads us with so many benefits.

This bit of poetry shall be my finish: I mean every word of it. Let us sing it together.

> "What pleasant groves, what goodly fields!
>   What fruitful hills and vales have we!
> How sweet an air our climate yields!
>   How blest with flocks and herds we be!
> How milk and honey doth o'erflow!
>   How clear and wholesome are our springs!
> How safe from ravenous beasts we go!
>   And, oh, how free from poisonous things!

"For these, and for our grass, our corn;
    For all that springs from blade or bough;
For all those blessings that adorn,
    Both wood and field, this kingdom through;
For all of these, thy praise we sing;
    And humbly, Lord, entreat thee too,
That fruit to thee we forth may bring,
    As unto us thy creatures do."

THE END

JOHN PLOUGHMAN'S TALK

or

PLAIN ADVICE
FOR PLAIN PEOPLE

In the simplest language the Author of *John Ploughman's Pictures*, presents a series of stories which go to the heart. Without offence being intended, some readers will be offended. If this results in a clearer understanding of problems discussed in story form, John Ploughman's purpose will have been served.